CAMBRIDGE LIBRARY COLLECTION

Books of enduring scholarly value

Egyptology

The large-scale scientific investigation of Egyptian antiquities by Western scholars began as an unintended consequence of Napoleon's invasion of Egypt during which, in 1799, the Rosetta Stone was discovered. The military expedition was accompanied by French scholars, whose reports prompted a wave of enthusiasm that swept across Europe and North America resulting in the Egyptian Revival style in art and architecture. Increasing numbers of tourists visited Egypt, eager to see the marvels being revealed by archaeological excavation. Writers and booksellers responded to this growing interest with publications ranging from technical site reports to tourist guidebooks and from children's histories to theories identifying the pyramids as repositories of esoteric knowledge. This series reissues a wide selection of such books. They reveal the gradual change from the 'tomb-robbing' approach of early excavators to the highly organised and systematic approach of Flinders Petrie, the 'father of Egyptology', and include early accounts of the decipherment of the hieroglyphic script.

Syria and Egypt

A pioneering Egyptologist, Sir William Matthew Flinders Petrie (1853–1942) excavated over fifty sites and trained a generation of archaeologists. In the early 1890s, he carried out significant work at Tell el-Amarna, the site of the ancient capital of Akhetaten. The illustrated 1894 excavation report that he co-authored has also been reissued in this series, along with many of his other publications. Petrie played a notable part in the preservation of a number of cuneiform tablets that became known collectively as the Tell el-Amarna letters. In this 1898 work, he presents summaries of the most important documents. They offer insights into war, peace and diplomacy in the Near East during the reigns of Amenhotep III and Akhenaten in the fourteenth century BCE. Informative notes on individuals and places mentioned in the letters help set them in context, while the methods used to interpret them are also elucidated.

T0370903

Cambridge University Press has long been a pioneer in the reissuing of out-of-print titles from its own backlist, producing digital reprints of books that are still sought after by scholars and students but could not be reprinted economically using traditional technology. The Cambridge Library Collection extends this activity to a wider range of books which are still of importance to researchers and professionals, either for the source material they contain, or as landmarks in the history of their academic discipline.

Drawing from the world-renowned collections in the Cambridge University Library and other partner libraries, and guided by the advice of experts in each subject area, Cambridge University Press is using state-of-the-art scanning machines in its own Printing House to capture the content of each book selected for inclusion. The files are processed to give a consistently clear, crisp image, and the books finished to the high quality standard for which the Press is recognised around the world. The latest print-on-demand technology ensures that the books will remain available indefinitely, and that orders for single or multiple copies can quickly be supplied.

The Cambridge Library Collection brings back to life books of enduring scholarly value (including out-of-copyright works originally issued by other publishers) across a wide range of disciplines in the humanities and social sciences and in science and technology.

Syria and Egypt

From the Tell el Amarna Letters

W.M. FLINDERS PETRIE

CAMBRIDGE
UNIVERSITY PRESS

CAMBRIDGE
UNIVERSITY PRESS

University Printing House, Cambridge, CB2 8BS, United Kingdom

Published in the United States of America by Cambridge University Press, New York

Cambridge University Press is part of the University of Cambridge.
It furthers the University's mission by disseminating knowledge in the pursuit of
education, learning and research at the highest international levels of excellence.

www.cambridge.org
Information on this title: www.cambridge.org/9781108065795

This edition first published 1898
This digitally printed version 2013

ISBN 978-1-108-06579-5 Paperback

SYRIA AND EGYPT

FROM THE TELL EL AMARNA LETTERS

SYRIA AND EGYPT

FROM THE TELL EL AMARNA
LETTERS

BY

W. M. FLINDERS PETRIE
D.C.L., LL.D., Ph.D., Hon. F.S.A. (Scot.)

METHUEN & CO.
36, ESSEX STREET, STRAND
LONDON
1898

CONTENTS

CONTENTS

SYRIA AND EGYPT

FROM THE

TELL EL AMARNA LETTERS

CHAPTER I.

INTRODUCTION

1. DURING the age of the decline of Egyptian power in Syria, when the great conquests of Tahutmes I. were all gradually lost, a splendid store of information was laid by for us in the cuneiform correspondence at Tell el Amarna. The clay tablets, mostly from Syria, but with a few duplicates of letters from Egypt, were deposited in "The place of the records of the palace of the king," as it is called upon the stamped bricks which I found still remaining there. A few years ago the natives, while plundering about the ruins and carrying off Akhenaten's bricks for their modern houses, lit upon this record chamber containing many hundreds of tablets. These were shown to dealers; they

B

sent some to Dr. Oppert, at Paris, who pro-
nounced them to be forgeries; others were
sent to M. Grebaut, then head of the Depart-
ment of Antiquities, and were treated by him
with customary silence. At last, when they
were supposed to be almost worthless, a
quantity were carried in sacks to Luqsor to
hawk about among the dealers there, and
these were largely ground to pieces on the
way. What has been preserved, therefore,
is but a wreck of what might have been, had
any person equal to the occasion placed his
hand upon them in time. The tablets thus
reaching the dealers' hands became known,
and were bought up mainly for the British
Museum and the Berlin Museum. Some
drifted to St. Petersburg, Paris, and the
Cairo Museums; and some into the private
collections of Murch, Rostowicz, and others.
A similar miserable fate attends all dis-
coveries in Egypt, unless made by a skilled
observer, as witness the palace of Ramessu
III. at Tell el Yehudiyeh, the Deir el Bahri
treasure, the cemetery of Ekhmim, the
palace of Amenhotep III. at Thebes, as
well as unnumbered cemeteries and towns
throughout the land.

The tablets thus dispersed were published

in many different ways and places; and the
first synopsis of the whole was given in the
second volume of my *History of Egypt*.
But since then a much larger number have
been published, with a more critical and
definitive text of the whole by Hugo
Winckler, in *The Tell el Amarna Letters*.
All the summaries of the letters which
I made before have been now revised with
Winckler's translations, and summaries of
all the new ones have been made from those
translations. I have retained the original
references to the older translations, because
Winckler's edition is so extremely bald and
deficient in general information, so purely
a linguistic exercise and not an effective
edition, that the older publications are still
of value for details of place, state, dockets,
&c. But in every case Winckler's number,
W. *n.*, is placed against each summary.

2. With regard to transliteration I have
departed from the system used by Winckler,
not without good reason. The rage for
employing out-of-the-way and little-known
symbols in place of effective letters which are
understood, threatens to place historical and
linguistic works as much outside of the
ordinary reader's pronunciation as a set of

chemical symbols or differential equations. When almost everything required can be expressed in commonly known terms, there is a pedantry about adopting what only specialists can read. Double letters, if in common use, are no real objection, as in the few cases where sh, th, kh, ts, &c., are really two separate letters, it is easy to put a hyphen between them to separate them. No mistake can thus arise; everyone can read and understand the names, and only the theoretic beauty of one letter, one sign, is interfered with. I accordingly use kh for kheth, th for teth, y for yod, s for samekh, ts for tsade, q for qoph, and sh for shin. When we may come to see Greek names written as Tales, Aḥilles, Pilippos, &c., it will be time enough to suppose that double letters are not wanted. In no possible case in any system should the sign j be used instead of y, as for the greater part of mankind it means a soft g, and the y sign cannot be misunderstood.

The summaries of each letter that are given here include every name of person or of place that occurs in the letter, every fact mentioned which can be of value for judging of the positions of persons or the conditions of affairs, and any presents or objects named. In short nothing is omitted but verbiage and phrases which are of no value for the history or the understanding of the position. The summaries are all that need to be compared and considered for their connections; yet in all important cases the full translations have been referred to here, when working out the history and geography, in order to make certain that no minute details were overlooked.

3. The order of the letters has been determined by dividing them into three main classes: (1) Royal letters and others during the peaceful times of Amenhotep III., and early in Amenhotep IV.; (2) the North Syrian war; (3) the South Syrian or Palestine war.

In the first class the letters of different places have no chronological interlocking, and therefore each kingdom and person is taken separately.

In the second class the main backbone of the sequence is in the history of Ribaddi; and in the third series the history of Abd-khiba (or Ebed-tob as formerly rendered) is the main sequence.

The first step was to place the letters of

each of these personal histories in the order of time, judging from the waning power of these allies of Egypt. The towns which they successively lost, and the difficulties in which they were, serve to fit the letters very closely together one after the other. The frequent changes of residence of Ribaddi have particularly to be noticed, as otherwise all the letters from one residence of his might be supposed to be earlier or later than those from another residence. No change of residence has been assumed here, except what is clearly required by the sequence of events that are named. In particular we may note the phrase, " May Baalat of Gubla give power to my lord the king." Such an invocation of the local deity might be supposed to show that the letter was written from Gubla. After settling the order and the locality of each letter of Ribaddi, as far as is shown by the evidence of events, then the invocations of the goddess of Gubla were tabulated. In most cases such letters appeared to have been written from Gubla. The results appear thus, the letters naming " Baalat of Gubla " or " Gubla your hand- maid " are thirty-two in all; of these, from the events, I classed :—

22 written in Gubla.
3 „   „ Berut.
7 early uncertain ones.
——

32 naming Gubla.

Of letters not naming Gubla in a gratuitous manner, there are twenty-five in all; of
these, from the events, I classed :—

11 written in Gubla.
10 „   „ Berut.
2 „   „ Tsumura.
2 early uncertain ones.
——

25 not naming Gubla.

Here, then, the test of the gratuitous
naming of Gubla is almost restricted to
letters written from Gubla, and it might
seem, therefore, that in three cases I had
made a mistake, in attributing three of this
class to Berut; but in one of these three we
have the positive proof that an invocation
of Baalat of Gebal might be written elsewhere, as Ribaddi says (No. 211, Winckler
62), "And behold at this time I am in
Berut." Hence I see no reason to change
to Gubla the venue of the other two letters.

The above test, therefore, is not conclusive; but it is interesting as showing that of the letters naming Gubla my arrangement only gives one in eight to other places; while of those not naming Gubla my arrangement gives more than half to other places. This is a perfectly unbiassed test, as it was not visible in the summaries which I arranged, and was never looked at in the letters until all the present arrangement was done.

4. Another matter to be noted is the change of allegiance of persons and places. Such change is always shown in the indices of persons and of places by a star; the references before the star (if any) being friendly to Egypt, the references after the star (if any) being hostile to Egypt. In many cases, however, there is a dubious period in which there are conflicting statements from different parties; in such cases the references that are dubious are placed between two stars. Such dubious references arise from several causes. Sometimes a man was misrepresented by his enemies in order to prejudice him in the opinion of the Egyptians. Sometimes an enemy of the Egyptians continued to claim to be on their

side as long as he could. But the more usual case seems to have been that the Egyptians had lost interest in Syria, lost the power of sparing troops to manage the country and to keep order, and lost heart in foreign matters since they were absorbed in the home politics of religious revolutions. So soon as the strong hand of the power of Egypt ceased to act in all emergencies, to interfere in every squabble, and to make capital out of the internal discords of the Syrians—so soon the Syrians began their old life of aggression one on the other. It was just what we see every year in India; any place without a garrison is liable to outbursts of the old feud of Hindu faith against Muhamedan. So it was in Syria; all the petty chiefs and shekhs whose ancestors had been cutting each other's throats for generations, and who, doubtless, had venerable blood-feuds unavenged, soon began to attack one another when not vigorously kept in hand by Egypt. Also any strong and capable man like Abdashirta and his son Aziru, soon found that he could safely bully his neighbours, and gradually acquire power over them.

Hence the weakening of Egypt threw

Syria into a state of internal discord un-
repressed. The immediate effect of this
was that various parties, without caring
particularly about being for or against the
Egyptians, began to fight with one another.
Each tried to draw the power of Egypt to
his own side by representing that he was
loyally acting in the interest of his suzerain ;
and the weaker party was sure to place his
trust most fully upon Egypt. It was only
when a man had played his own hand for
a long time, had strengthened himself by
absorbing much of his neighbour's goods
and lands, and had safely neglected the
orders of the Egyptians on several occa-
sions—it was only then that he cared to
throw off the mask and act openly in his
own interest, and allow himself to be classed
as an enemy. Hence we often find very
different views of people, and might put
them as being on the Egyptian side according to their own account long after they
were on the enemies' side according to other
accounts.

5. A very important consideration which
has not been worked out hitherto lies in
the few chronological details which can be
gathered. It is obvious that excepting a

small proportion of peaceful letters under Amenhotep III., all the rest of these record the downfall of Egyptian power under Akhenaten. It is possible to glean some indications, however, of a more exact dating, and to allot the main outlines to their approximate years.

In the Mitanni letters up to No. 8 they are to Amenhotep III., No. 9 is to the IVth.

In the Kardunyash letters up to No. 17 they are to Amenhotep III., No. 18 is to the IVth.

In the letter from an unknown king to the kings of Kinakhi (No. 40) condolences on the death of a king, evidently Amenhotep III., are named. In letter 123 is a reference to the 3rd year, which cannot be any but the year of Amenhotep IVth, and must have been written later, as his father did not die till the 5th year of his son's reckoning. At this time caravans seem to have been freely passing.

Two important letters (111, 112), of Akizzi of Qatna, near Damascus, addressed to Amenhotep III., show that serious troubles were in progress before his death, probably in the last year or two, the 4th

and 5th year of Amenhotep IVth's joint
reign. The political prospect then was that
Nukhashi, Ni, Zinzar, and Kinanat (or the
Upper Orontes) were still faithful, but
in danger. The Damascus plain was
seriously threatened. The Lower Orontes,
or Amurra, was already in revolt under
Azira, and the Khatti were hostile.

From this point we may approximately
start the reckoning of Azira's wars and
attacks on Ribaddi, say in the 5th year of
Amenhotep IV., the epoch of letter 140,
when Ribaddi first asks for troops to defend
himself from Abdashirta and the Khabiri.

In letter 174 we read that Ribaddi had
fought for five years, bringing this point to
about the 10th year of Akhenaten.

Then in letter 186 Ribaddi's son had been
sent from Berut to see the king, but had not
succeeded in doing so for three months.
About a year must be allowed to this point,
or the 11th year.

In letter 204 Ribaddi complains that
Gubla has been besieged for three years,
causing famine, owing to the cutting off of
the arable land. As the complaints of the
trouble of Gubla begin in letter 187, this
three years will date from about then, so

that letter 204 will be at least as late as the 14th year.

In the tomb of Huya, No. 1, at Tell el Amarna, there are prisoners of the Kharu; and this tomb shows only two figures of princesses which are, therefore, about the 7th–8th year, and contains a date of the 12th year. The carvings occupied some time therefore, and the prisoners may well refer to some successes which Ribaddi seems to have had about the 12th year, when in letter 192 he anticipates being able to drive out Azira. We therefore have approximate dates of

		B.C. about.
Letter 111, 112—4th, 5th year Akhenaten		
(end of Amenhotep III.) .	.	1379
„ 123, referring to 3rd year, but after		
4th year	.	1379
„ 140, 5th year (?) of Akhenaten	.	1378
„ 174, 10th year (?) . . .	.	1373
„ 186, 11th year (?) . . .	.	1372
„ 193, 12th year (?) . . .	.	1371
„ 204, 14th year (?) . . .	.	1369
„ 225, 17th year (? ?) end of Ri-		
baddi	.	1366

6. The questions of the positions of the various places named in these letters require to be systematically treated and not dealt

with by a hap-hazard system of verbal coincidence.

That such has been far too much the case can be seen in one well-known instance. The king of Megiddo had three country palaces, or storehouses, which were plundered by the Egyptians immediately after the fall of Megiddo, in the 23rd year of Tahutmes III. (*History* ii. 110); they were named Yenuamu, Anaugasa, and Harnekaru. From the history it is plain that they were within the kingdom ruled from Megiddo, and not far away therefore, and that they were not on the Egyptian side of Megiddo. Yet, in face of this, the astounding identification of the kingdom of Nukhashi, far in the north, for the store city of Anaugasa, and the city of Rhinocolura, far to the south, for the store city of Harnekaru, have been gravely upheld in defiance of all geography. When we look, on the reasonable grounds of apparent position, to the region a little north of Megiddo, we there see Yanuh, or Yenu of the Amu up one valley, and Nakura (with Ras en Nakura, the hill or Har-nakura by it) up another valley, and possibly even the third name Anaugasa surviving in an intermediate valley where a ruin is called Medinet en Nehas.

Though the positions must thus be the first consideration in fixing places, yet we must not go to the opposite extreme and say that names cannot be trusted, and that nothing can be certain. When we see the names of Akka, Askaluna, Biruta, Danuna, Gazri, Lakish, Qideshu, Timasgi, Tsiduna, Tsurri, Tsumura, Tunip, Urushalim, Yapu, and Zinzar, all lasting with no change—or only a small variation in vowels—down to the present day, when nearly all the most important places might be named in cuneiform to the modern peasant, it needs no further proof that ancient names may be safely sought for in the modern map. Altogether, out of about 150 names of places in these letters, about 100 can be fixed with more or less certainty, and many of the others might probably be found if there were indications of the district in which to seek them.

The practical method followed in preparing the lists of places, and the map, has been to extract from the letters every mention of a place, with all other places which are mentioned with it, then by means of the other names to delimit what may be the possible ground for the unknown name. Next, considering the usual mutations between the transcription of cuneiform and the modern Arabic forms, to frame the shape in which it would be most likely to occur; and then to search the maps by reading over every name within the possible limits.

In dealing with names there are several sources of divergence between the cuneiform transcription and modern Arabic. The name may have been variable in form anciently, as some names now are; it may have been changed in being transcribed into cuneiform; it may have changed during over three thousand years and many conquests; or it may have been changed on being transcribed into Arabic. Thus there are so many possibilities of change, which actually occur in many cases, that we may wonder at the principal places having preserved their names so closely as they have done. In identifying names another consideration is in the descriptive nature of many of them. In the present list we meet with 'Amq, the valley or deep place; Ginti, the gardens; Kirmil, the vineyard; Gubla or Gebal, the rock or mountain; Kharabu, the ruin; Magdali, a tower; Rubuta, a capital; and Yarimuta, the Yerimoth or high place. Being descriptive, such might be easily found repeated, and hence there is the more need to look fully at the indications of locality in fixing such names.

7. The references to the published sources of the letters are given not only to the latest and fullest edition by Winckler (W), *The Tell el Amarna Letters*, but also to the earlier publications which are accompanied by more details as to the place, state, &c., of the tablets. These are indicated thus:— R.P. xiii.-xviii., *Records of the Past*, series ii., vols. i.–vi. S.B.A., *Proceedings of the Society of Biblical Archæology.* M.A.F., *Mission Archeologique Française.* B.O.D. Bezold, *Oriental Diplomacy*, and the *Tell el Amarna Tablets*, same numbers. P.A., Petrie, *Tell el Amarna.* But in all cases the summary follows the latest edition by Winckler.

8. Before entering upon these letters it will be well to give a sketch of the previous relations of Egypt to Syria, which explain the position of affairs at the time when this correspondence begins. Before the XVIIIth Dynasty the Egyptians had not much relation with the East. The kings of the IVth

c

Dynasty had a fighting frontier as near home as in Sinai; the Vth Dynasty carried the war further east among the Sati, and besieged and took fortified cities of theirs, as shown at Deshasheh. The XIIth Dynasty fought the Sati, as named by Amenemhat I., and figured on the pectorals of Usertesen III. and Amenemhat III. The independence of all Southern Syria is evident from the history of Sanehat, where it does not appear that the Egyptians had an occupation beyond the Isthmus of Suez.

It was not until the rolling back of the tide of the conquering Syrians, in the expulsion of the Hyksos, that the Egyptians took any permanent hold outside of their own land. Aahmes, in the first rush of conquest, reached as far as Zahi, or the middle of the Syrian coast. Amenhotep I. seems to have done nothing in Syria, occupied probably in the consolidation and prosperity of Egypt. Tahutmes I. conquered the whole length of Syria as far as the Euphrates, having set up his tablet of victory at Naharaina or northern Mesopotamia. Tahutmes III. did as much, but no more. Amenhotep II. seems to have lost ground, as he found in his young days an enemy to repulse at Harosheth, on the

Kishon, just beyond Carmel. Tahutmes IV. fought the Khita, who must at that time have been far in the north, up to Cilicia, and hence he seems to have occupied the whole of Syria.

Of Amenhotep III.—the first king of this correspondence — there are, unfortunately, very few records of his conquests or power. For the names of the subject peoples of Syria we are dependent on the decorative figures of captives around the columns of the temple at Soleb in Ethiopia. There are three series of them, each series double ; part facing one way and part the other. The most probable order to read them is from the pair face to face, reading first those which face to right and then those which face to left. The series then appear thus (see *Leps. Denk.* iii. 88) :

FIRST SERIES.

Sengar	Singara, W. of Nineveh.
Naharain	Upper Euphrates, both sides.
Khita	N. end of Syria, Comagene.
——	——
Kedesh	By Lake Homs ?
Tanepu	Tunip, Tennib.
(lost)	?
(lost)	?

Akarita   .   Ugarit, mouth of Orontes.
Kefa   .   N. Phœnicia.

SECOND SERIES.

Karkamish   Karkhamish.
Asur   .   Assyria.
Apththena   Aphadana, 35° 30', E. of Chaboras.
         or Aphphadana, 34° 35', E. of Euphrates.
——— .
Makuuatsh   Maguda, 35° 40', E. of Euphrates.
Mehpeni, or   ?
Shedpeni ?

THIRD SERIES.

Kedina   .   Katanii, E. of Palmyra.
Aaro, or
Atiro ?   .   Atera, 45' S, 20' W., of Palmyra.
——— .
Pah . . .   ?
Punt   .   Punda, about 31°, W. of Euphrates.
Sha . u   .   Shasu? Bedawin.
Thyta   .   ?
Arerpaka .   Arrapakhitis, N.E. of Nineveh.

In the first series there is the extreme
north of Syria, and then the north-central
and round to northern coast. For the place
of Ugarit see the discussion farther on. In
the second series we begin on the Upper
Euphrates and go down the valley. In the
third series there is the Palmyra desert,

and then the Lower Euphrates and up to Nineveh. The name Aaro is unlikely, and probably one of the *a* birds is really *ti*, as these are often confounded : it would then read Atiro, and so may well be Atera near Palmyra. The name Punt occurring here with a strongly-marked Syrian figure, and next to the Shasu, was a stumbling-block, until the possibility was noticed of its being really eastern, in accord with the figure and position, and representing Punda on the Lower Euphrates. This name of Ptolemy is variable, reading also Gunda and Spunda. The Shasu are well known as Bedawin in general. Thyta is the next name, not identified with any place; it seems barely possible that it was the land of Queen Thy, named after her by the Egyptians, and that it would read " Thy's land." Lastly, Arer-paka is Arapkha of the Assyrians, Arra-pakhitis of the Greeks, a district just north of Nineveh.

These lists show that Amenhotep III., either by conquest or by treaty, had extended even the empire which had been acquired by Tahutmes I. and III. The whole Euphra-tes appears to be subject to him, down to 31° N., the Tigris up to Assyria and Arra-

pakhitis, and the Palmyra desert between
Syria and Mesopotamia. This shows apparently the greatest extent of the Egyptian
power ever known; in classical terms it
comprised the whole of Syria, Mesopotamia,
Chaldea, and Assyria, stopping only at the
frontiers of Susiana, Media, and Armenia.

It is now the breaking up of all this
power that we have detailed before us in the
letters from Tell el Amarna. Much had
been already lost in the later years of
Amenhotep III.; in letters 111, 112 the
governor of Qatna near Damascus states
that Azira, the centre of North Syrian independence, was in revolt, the Khatti were
at war, and places round Damascus were
rebelling. Yet up to the close of the reign
of the third Amenhotep and beginning of the
fourth, the letters passed regularly to and from
Babylonia and northern Mesopotamia, so
that no serious break of communications had
taken place. The serious overthrow belongs
to the reign of Akhenaten, when, having
openly broken with all the traditions of his
Amenhotep youth, he threw all his energies
into domestic reform, and abandoned foreign
politics with disastrous results. It was not
till a generation later, under Horemheb, that

the Egyptians again obtained a hold on Syria. Even the boasted conquests of Sety I. and Ramessu II. did not more than half recover the length of Syria ; while they did not attempt alliances with Mesopotamia and Babylonia, but were content to meekly make treaties on equal terms with the Khita, who had absorbed the greater part of Syria, and who had laid out that kingdom which was so familiar to the Israelites.

In later times the warlike Merenptah, Ramessu III. and Sheshenq I., claimed authority again over Palestine, but they did not venture to go beyond the Ramesside territory. In the XXVIth Dynasty Nekau (Necho) struck boldly through Syria to the Euphrates, only to be defeated at Carchemish ; and the Ptolemies, though holding Cyprus and much of Phœnicia, yet did not succeed in acquiring the Seleucid kingdom of Antioch. At no period, therefore, can we place the power of Egypt higher than it was under Amenhotep III., lord of the two great cradles of civilization, the narrow valley of Nile, and the plains and highlands of Mesopotamia.

9. *Positions of Principal Personages named.*

Abdashirta of Amurra &c. (Orontes valley).
Abdkhiba of Jerusalem.
Abimilki of Tyre.
Addumikhir of Gaza.
Akizzi of Qatana.
Amanappa, commissioner.
Amunira of Beyrut.
Artamaniya of Bashan.
{ Arzauni of Rukhizi.
{ Arzawiya of Mikhizi.
Assur-nadinakhi } kings of Assyria.
Assur-uballidh }
Aziri of Amurra, &c.
Bikhura, commissioner in Kamid.
Biridya of Megiddo.
Burnaburyash of Babylonia.
Dushratta of Mitani.
Itakama of Kinza and Qedesh.
Kallimasin of Babylonia.
Khaib, commissioner of Simyra.
Khatib, commissioner.
Lapaya in S. Palestine.
Milkili in S. Palestine.
Namiawiza of Kamid.
Ninur of Seffin.
Pakhura (see Bikhura).
Puaddi of Yerza.
Raman-nirari of Nukhashi.
Rabimur } of Gubla, &c.
Ribaddi }

Shumadda of Merom.
Shutatna of Akko.
Suwarzana of 'Azziyeh.
Tarkhundaraush, king of Hittites.
Tiuwatti of Helbon.
Yabiteri of Gaza and Joppa.
Yabni-il of Lachish.
Yankhamu, commissioner.
Yapa-addi, commissioner.
Yapakhi of Gezer.
Yitya of Askelon.
Zimrida of Lachish.
Zimrida of Zidon.
Zitatna (see Shutatna).

CHAPTER II.

LETTERS OF THE PEACE

10. *Kings of the Khatti.*

An early letter to Amenhotep III. cannot be regularly translated, as it is in an unknown language, but a few names can be transliterated and may lead to some results. From the personal name it would seem that the sender was a Hittite king, the word *Tarkhun* being well known in the name of the king Tarqu-dimme of the silver boss, the same name as the king Tarkondemos of Greek times. From the letter can be gleaned the following :—

(1) TARKHUNDARAUSH to NIMUTRIYA. (Amenhotep III.) T. sends Irshappa for a daughter of N. ; and sends a *shuka* of gold, and will send a chariot, &c. Prince of the Khatti on the mountains of Igaid sends a *shuka* weighing 20 manehs, 3 *kak* of ivory, 3 *kak* of *pirkar*, 3 *kak* of *khuzzi*, 8 *kak* of *kusittiu*, 100 *kak* of lead, 5 *kukupu* stones, 10 thrones of *usu* wood, 2 *usu* trees.   (S.B.A. xi. 336.)

The throne name of Amenhotep III., which we render as Neb-maat-ra, was variously vocalized by the cuneiform scribes as Nimmuria, Nammuria, Nimutriya, or Mimmuria; these variations show how little exactness can be expected in cuneiform versions of names.

The reference to the mountain of Igaid is a clue, as that is apparently the Ygatiy of the Travels of the Mohar of Ramesside times; and from the position of the name there it seems to have been about the Lebanon, perhaps connected with *Ain Yakut* on the old pass over the Lebanon, between Damascus and Beyrut. So this prince of the Khatti ruled on the Lebanon in the time of Amenhotep III., showing how the Hittites had already begun to occupy Syria. The Hittite writer of the letter seems to have been entering on the family alliances with the Egyptians, which were carried on till Ramessu II. Another letter appears to be also from the Hittites, showing that they were tributaries, or, at least, on good terms.

(2) ZIDA . . . to king of Egypt. When messengers went to the Khatti, Z. alone sent

presents; and now he sends 16 boys, and asks for gold in return.

(Winckler 36; S.B.A. xiii. 132.)

Another letter has been supposed to be from a king of the Khatti, but Winckler does not accept this from the fragment of the name, . . . *ti.*

(3) King of (KHA)TTI to KHURI (short for Nipkhuriya, Amenhotep IV.). Asks for an alliance, as between their fathers. Sends a *bibru* of silver, 5 minas, another 3 minas, 2 *gaggaru* of silver, 10 minas, and 2 great *nikibtu.*   (W. 35; S.B.A. xiii. 549.)

11. *Dushratta of Mitani.*

The principal series of letters which show family relationships between the Egyptian kings and those of Syria are those sent by Dushratta, king of Mitani, to Amenhotep III. and IV. The earliest of these refers to the accession of Dushratta, and to his troubles from the invasion of the Khatti. The land of Mitani, in the north of Mesopotamia, bordering on the Euphrates, was close to the Hittite country, and would be naturally in the way of their attacks.

(4) DUSHRATTA to NIPMUARIA (Amenhotep III.).   D. greets Gilukhipa his sister.
Soon after his accession Pirkhi attacked his
land and his people; but D. repulsed him,
and slew the murderers of D.'s brother
Artash-shumara, whom P. supported.   D.
notifies N. of this, as N. was a friend of
D.'s father, who gave him D.'s sister.   The
Khatti came into D.'s land, but D.'s god,
Tishub, gave them into his hand.   D. sends
a chariot, 2 horses, a lad, and a girl, of the
booty of the Khatti.   Also 5 chariots and
pairs of horses.   Also to D.'s sister Gilukhipa a pair of breast ornaments of gold, a
pair of earrings of gold, a *mash-hu* of gold,
and a jar of oil.   D. sends Gilia a messenger
and Tunip-ipri.   Let N. return them soon.
(W. 16; S.B.A. xv. 120.)

(5) DUSHRATTA to NIMMURIYA.   N. sent
Mani to ask for daughter of D. to be
mistress of Egypt.   Giliya, D.'s messenger,
reported words of N. which rejoiced D.
And D. asks much gold, as N. sent to his
father Shutarna a dish, cup, and brick of
solid gold.   D. sends Giliya, and a present
of a gold goblet set with lazuli; a necklace
of 20 lazuli beads and 19 of gold, in middle
lazuli cased in gold; a necklace of 42
khulalu stones, and 40 gold beads; and an
amulet of *khulalu* stone in gold, 10 pairs of
horses, 10 chariots of wood, and 30 women.
(W. 17; R.P. xv. 84.)

Here Dushratta is sending grand presents, besides being willing to give up a daughter to Egypt. This points to his being a tributary, and not entirely independent. Amenhotep III. sends an envoy to negotiate for a princess to be the "mistress of Egypt," and this was not for himself, but for his son, as the later letters show. To Dushratta's letter above, Amenhotep replied by accepting the present, and sending again to fetch the princess. His request is acknowledged in the next letter, while the princess was preparing for the journey.

(6) DUSHRATTA to NIMMURIYA. Mani, A.'s messenger, has come to fetch a wife from D. to be the mistress of Egypt. Land of Khani-galbat, and land of Egypt will live in peace . . . After 6 months Giliya and Mani were now sent with the queen. Kharamashi sent by D. with letter. D. asks for much gold; has sent an *ushu* stone, an *isizzu* of Aleppo stone, and a *khulal* stone set in gold.

(W. 18; R.P. xv. 74.)

In the next letter Dushratta calls himself father-in-law to Amenhotep III., referring to some previous marriage, and not to the one just negotiated, as this last was of

Amenhotep IV., as shown by letters 9, 10, 11. Two other letters to Amenhotep IV. refer to the family relationships.

(7) DUSHRATTA to NIMMURIYA. D. is father-in-law to N. May Istar bless N. Mani the messenger, and Khani, dragoman of N., have brought presents; D. sends lazuli and some gold.

(W. 19; R.P. xv. 73.)

(8) DUSHRATTA to NIMMURIYA. D. greets Tadukhipa his daughter and Nimmuriya his son-in-law. Sends statue of Istar of Nina to be honoured by N. and returned.

(W. 20; S.B.A. xv. 124.)

On the back of this is an hieratic docket, apparently in the 36th year of Amenhotep III., month of Pharmuthi. This is the very latest date in the reign, and would be two or three weeks later than the papyrus of Kahun dated under Amenhotep IV. Possibly in the last illness of Amenhotep III. the dating under his co-regent son came into use irregularly, and in any case official correspondence of the palace would receive the date of the king to whom it was addressed. By its date this must be the last letter of this reign.

After the death of Amenhotep III.,

Amenhotep IV. was but a youth of about
18 years old; and hence Dushratta hesitated
at addressing confidential diplomacy to him,
and wrote in the first place to Queen Tyi.
As we already know, from a quarry inscrip-
tion at Tell el Amarna, this queen was for
a short time apparently sole regent. Tyi
appears from the following letter to have
acted as regent independently of her son,
and to have taken the position of sending
out the diplomatic messengers to keep up
the relation with foreign states.

(9) DUSHRATTA to TEIE. D. greets Teie
her son, and Tadukhipa his bride. Appeals
to friendship with Mimmuria (Amenhotep
III.), and Teie knows all the negotiations
better than the messengers Gilia and Mani.
Asks that certain gold statues be sent, along
with presents to Yuni, D.'s wife.
(W. 22; S.B.A. xv. 127.)

Gilia was the messenger of Dushratta, and
was sent back with the news of the death of
Amenhotep III., and a request for continu-
ance of friendship. Hence he must have
arrived just about the time of the king's
death, and was therefore the bearer of letter
8, which came just at that time. This letter
9 is Dushratta's next after No. 8.

(10) DUSHRATTA to NAPKHURIRIA (Amenhotep IV.).   To N. my brother, my son-in-law, D. your father-in-law, your brother: salutations to N.'s mother Teie, to D.'s daughter, Tadukhipa, N.'s other wives, sons, &c.   Pirizzi and Bubri were sent by D. to condole with N.   Mani N.'s messenger was kept by D. until the return of D.'s messenger.   Teie knows all past discussions, and N. must consult her.

(W. 24 ; M.A.F. vi. 304 ; R.P. xv. 89.)

The name of Amenhotep IV., Neferkheperu-ra, was rendered in cuneiform as Napkhuriria. This letter is conclusive as to Tadukhipa being daughter of Dushratta and wife of Amenhotep IV. On no monuments is there any trace of any other wife of the king, and from the great prominence of Nefertiti, Akhenaten's devotion to her, and the absence of any children but hers (although all of hers were daughters), it seems that Nefertiti must be this wife Tadukhipa. It is true that Dushratta also greets other wives of Amenhotep IV., which would imply several such ; but he also greets sons, whereas there is no trace of any son, and had there been one it is unlikely that he would have been ignored and only a long string of daughters put forward. The

D

phrase, therefore, of "wives and sons" is merely a conventional presumption.

The next letter is the longest of the whole series, about 190 lines in all, filling over eight octavo pages even in its defective condition. It begins with the same relationships as the previous letter, therefore omitted here.

(11) DUSHRATTA to NAPKHURIA. From D.'s youth Nimmuria wrote to him, and Teie knows all that passed. When Nimmuria's father (Tahutmes IV.) sent to Artatama, D.'s grandfather, for his daughter, she was only granted at the 7th application. Nimmuria sent to Shutarna, D.'s father, for D.'s sister, who was only granted at the 6th application. Nimmuria sent to D. for D.'s daughter, and D. sent her, with an exchange of presents, by Khamashi (Kha-em-uas), N.'s messenger. And Nimmuria rejoiced in Tadukhipa. Gilia was D.'s agent in exchanges, and Nizag was N.'s agent. Nimmuria promised D. to make gold of Egypt plentiful in Khanigalbat; so D. asks for golden images. D. describes his grief at Nimmuria's death. Mani was Nimmuria's messenger. D. sent Perizzi and Bubri to condole. D.'s present messenger is Mazipalali, uncle of Gilia. D. has imprisoned Artishub and Asali who attacked

Egyptian territory. D. sends presents for Teie and for Tadukhipa.

(W. 21 ; R.P. xv. 79.)

This letter is very important as showing the long-standing relationships between the Mitanian kings and the Egyptian : it gives also the names of Dushratta's father, Shutarna, and grandfather, Artatama. The difference should be noted, that these two earlier kings only yielded a daughter to the Egyptian king after many applications, whereas Dushratta says that he yielded at one bargain. This agrees well to Amenhotep III. having much extended the frontiers of Egypt; in earlier reigns the Euphrates was the boundary, and frontier neighbours, such as Mitani, were independent, but after Amenhotep III. had absorbed all Mesopotamia and Assyria, the king of Mitani was his vassal and had to agree with all decent dignity to his proposals.

The last letter of this series touches on much the same lines, so that we must regard all these three letters as having been written within a short time. Thus this correspondence with Mitani must have been cut off by Aziru's attacks which began in the north

within the first year or two of the reign of
Amenhotep IV.

(12) DUSHRATTA to NAPKHURI.   Mani,
N.'s messenger, has come.   N. desired that
as D. had been friends with his father,
Mimmuria, so D. should be with N.   D.
will be ten times more so.   M. sent Mani to
D. with the price for a wife.   M. promised
golden images, lazuli, and instruments and
much gold, but N. has not sent them.
Khamashi took message from N.   Names
Gilia and Perizzi. (W. 23 ; S.B.A. xiii. 556.)

Both Mani and Khamassi were employed
by Amenhotep III. as messengers.   It is
clear that these letters were written with a
full appreciation of business.   The marriages
are always connected with large gifts ; presents are always sent, or expected, through
the messengers, and the kings of Mitani
were quite familiar with all the oriental ways
of politely screwing a present or a promise
out of their friends.   We can hardly doubt
that the Egyptian letters were of the same
kind, but we have only one copy of a
letter to royalty, and a few letters to in-
feriors.

12. *Kallimasin of Babylonia.*

Beside the alliance with Mitani, the north-western end of Mesopotamia nearest to Asia Minor, there was a similar alliance with Southern Mesopotamia or Babylonia, then known as Karduniyash. The successive kings of this region were Karaindash, Kalli-masin, Kurigalzu, and Burnaburyash, who is the best known.

(13) NIBMUARIA to KALLIMA-SIN, king of Karduniyash. N. (Amenhotep III.) had asked for a princess from K. But K. complained that his sister, who had been given to N. by K.'s father, had not been seen again. N. complains that K. never sent a messenger who could recognize his sister. Riqa, the messenger of Zaqara, was sent. K. complained that his messengers could not tell if the queen shown to them was a daughter of a beggar, or of Gagaia, or Khanigalbat, or Ugarit. But if K. doubts in this way, does he demand likewise tokens from all the other kings to whom his daughters are married? And N. is angry that K.'s messengers complain about not receiving gifts, when they always have presents given to them. N. asks that the messengers be not believed, as they plot treachery. K. said that N. had put his

chariots among those of the vassals, so that
K.'s agent could not find them.   But both
agent and chariots belong to K., and N. has
no horses to spare.   K. employs Riqa to
write.   (W. 1 ; S.B.A. xv. 26.)

The last sentence seems to mean that N.
had no need of K.'s chariots, and his agent
might as well take possession of them;
and if K. was so particular N. had no
horses to give in exchange.   It is evident
that the distance made communication
troublesome, and both parties became too
particular about being satisfied, so that there
was a good deal of ill-feeling.   But the
representations and assurances of Amenhotep III. seem to have satisfied Kallimasin,
for he promised to send a daughter.

(14) KALLIMASIN to NIMMUWARIA.   K.'s
daughter, whom N. asked for, is grown up
and will be sent.   N.'s father used to return
a messenger quickly, but N. has kept the
messenger for six years, and then only sent
30 minas of gold like silver, tested before
Kasi, N.'s messenger.   K. sends 35 male
slaves and 15 female as a present.
(W. 2 ; S.B.A. xiii. 130.)

The large present of slaves sent, after such
a small return from Egypt, seems as if

Babylonia was practically tributary to Amenhotep III., and so agrees to his representing
places in that region as his subjects. Yet
the king could ask plainly for return presents,
as in the next letter, which is apparently from
him, though the names are lost.

(15) *x* to *y*. *x* refers to a former request and
refusal of a daughter of the Egyptian king
for any foreign prince. *x* then said he would
take any beautiful Egyptian, and who should
say, "She is not a king's daughter"? *x*
asks for gold, either in Tammuz or Ab, and
he will send his daughter to *y*; he wants the
gold to finish work then, and if not sent by
that time he will not accept even 3000
talents of gold.   (W. 3; S.B.A. xiii. 128.)

Another letter refers to a sending of an
Egyptian princess, and the presents sent to
Egypt in return.

(16) KALLIMASIN to NIBMUARIA. K. sends
necessaries for N.'s house to return by the
messenger Shuti who brings N.'s daughter,
even a couch of *ushu* wood, ivory, and gold,
three couches and six thrones of *ushu* and
gold, an object of 7 minas of silver, and 9
shekels of gold, and other furniture.
(W. 5; B.O.D. 4.)

And a fragment of a letter has some references to marriages and presents.

(17) KALIMMASIN to NIMUWARIA. Greetings, and mentions "my daughters," and a few words relating to presents.   (W. 4.)

13. *Burnaburyash of Babylonia.*

The death of Kallimasin seems to have occurred very closely at the same time as that of Amenhotep III., as none of his letters are addressed to the IVth; and none of the letters of Burraburiash, his successor, are addressed to the IIIrd. One of the first letters, apparently, is a short one mainly desiring continued alliance.

(18) BURRABURIASH to NAPKHURURIA. Let N. write and ask for what he wants and B. will send it.   (W. 6.)

Next we see an active interchange going on between the kings.

(19) BURRABURIASH to NAPKHURARIA. From the times of Karaindash, since N.'s father's messengers came to B.'s father, they have been friendly. N.'s messengers have thrice come without presents. When 20 minas of gold were sent it was short weight and when smelted did not amount to 5 minas.

B. offers furs; and if they are spoiled by keeping, let Shindishugab, the messenger, hasten
to bring the chariots in order to get fresh
furs.   B. sends 2 minas of *uknu* stone ; and
for N.'s daughter, wife of B.'s son, a necklace
of 1048 stones.   (W. 8 ; S.B.A. xv. 117.)

The daughter of N., being the wife of B.'s
son, can only possibly refer to a betrothal, as
this letter cannot be later than the 8th or
10th year of Akhenaten at the latest, and
hence his daughters were none over six years
old at the time.

Another letter·refers to the subject of the
earlier letter (15) of Kallimasin.   In that
letter the king was very anxious to get gold
to decorate a work of his, and here we see
that a temple was being adorned, and much
gold was needed for it.

(20) BURRABURIASH to NIPKHURIRIA.
       Their fathers were allies, and sent presents,
       but now N. has sent only 2 minas of gold.
       " The work on the Temple is great, and
       vigorously have I undertaken its accomplish-
       ment ; send me therefore much gold."   In
       time of B.'s father Kurigalzu, the Kinakhaiu
       sent to him to attack Egyptians, but K.
       threatened to attack them in that case.   B.
       desires that the Ashuraiu should not be
       allowed to trade with Egypt.   Presents

sent: 3 minas of lazuli, 5 pair of horses, and 5 wooden chariots.

(W. 7; S.B.A. xiii. 540; R.P. xv. 63.)

In another letter the temple work again comes in as a claim for gold, apparently less urgently, and therefore later.

(21) BURNABURIASH to NAPKHURURIA. N.'s father complained, and B. sent Khuaa, and wrote promising another daughter; and N. has sent Khamashshi . . . . and Mikhuni. . . . B. will send daughter with 5 chariots, but fears king will scoff, as his father sent B.'s sister with 3000 men. Asks for Tsalma as commissioner. Khay who was sent had no chariot or people with him. Send many people, and Khay will bring B.'s daughter. N.'s father sent much gold to Kurigalzu. B. sends lazuli; and to queen only 20 stones of lazuli, as she neglected him. Asks for more gold to finish his temple. (W. 9.)

Another letter from the same king seems to be the latest during the peace, as there has been an illness of the king. There is no mention of the temple affairs which he took over from his predecessor, and the caravans are beginning to be plundered.

(22) BURRABURIASH to NAPKHURURIA.
B. unwell, and annoyed at N. not condoling.
Messenger explains distance to account for
N.'s silence. Sends 4 minas blue stone and
5 pair of horses. Asks for much gold, last
was base, because N. did not see to it
himself, and much loss in melting. Caravan
of Tsalmu B.'s messenger twice plundered
—1. By Biriamaza; 2. By Pamakhu, in N.'s
land—so asks for compensation to Tsalmu.

(W. 10.)

The last letter of all from Karduniash will
be found later on, No. 124, as it belongs to
the beginning of the northern wars, and
throws light on the persons involved in those
troubles. This correspondence was not
limited entirely to official business, but the
princesses took advantage of the messengers
to exchange affectionate greetings with their
families; probably many such went, though,
as they would not be likely to be kept in
official archives, only three have come down
to us.

(23) "Daughter of the king, to my lord . . . may
the gods of Burraburiash go with you.
Go out in peace, and in peace return to
your house." Sent by Kidin-Ramman.

(W. 13.)

(24) To . . . . my mistress . . . . khipa your handmaid. At the feet of my mistress I fall. Health to my mistress. . . .

(W. 292.)

(25) To . . . . my mistress, your daughter, your handmaid. At the feet of my mistress seven times and seven times I fall. . . .

(W. 293.)

14. *King of Alashia.*

A third series of royal letters are those from Alashia, which by a docket in hieratic upon one of them is identified with the Egyptian Alasa. It has been usually supposed that this was in the north of Syria, but Winckler's identification of it with Cyprus seems much more likely. Every letter refers to sending quantities of copper to Egypt, copper being commonly worked in Cyprus, but not on the mainland; silver is asked for in return, whereas silver was common among North Syrian Hittites; the ships of Alashia go to Egypt, whereas none of the Syrian ships are named there; all of these details point to Cyprus. And also Alashia was on the route followed from Gubla to Egypt, see letter 161.

(26) King of ALASHIA to king of Egypt. Congratulates him on his accession, sends

200 talents of copper, desires messenger
back quickly, and a yearly embassy each
way.   (W. 30.)

(27) King of ALASHIA to king of Egypt. E.
had enquired why a messenger had not
come. A. did not know that E. was
celebrating a sacrificial feast. A. now
sends a messenger with 100 talents of
copper. Asks for a couch of *ushu* wood
gilded, a gilded chariot, two horses, 42
garments, 50 . . . garments, 24 logs of
ushu wood, 17 boxes of good oil. . . .
Proposes a bond of alliance, and interchange of messengers. Sends a flask of
good oil to pour on E.'s head " now that
you have ascended the throne of your
kingdom."   (W. 27 ; B.O.D. 6.)

(28) *x* to *y*, sends ivory, 5 talents of copper, 3
talents of good copper, and *ushu* wood, and
desires that the customs officers shall not
interfere with the men sent in the ship.
                           (W. 33 ; S.B.A. xi. 340.)

(29) King of ALASHIA to king of Egypt. Asks
for return of messengers quickly, and says
they are his merchants, and desires that the
customs officer shall not interfere with them
or their ship.
                   (W. 29 ; S.B.A. xi. 334 ; xiii. 547.)

This bears a docket in hieratic " Letter
from Alasa." These letters show the marine

trade that was being carried on from Alashia.

(30) King of ALASHIA to king of Egypt. Sends 5 talents of copper and 5 pair of horses. Asks for silver. Desires messenger back soon, and mentions Pashtummi, Kunia, Itilluna, Ushbarra, and Bil-ram.   (W. 26.)

(31) King of ALASHIA to king of Egypt. Protests that the king of Egypt is mistaken in supposing the Alashians to be allied with the Lukki; on the contrary the Lukki yearly plunder the city of Zikhra in Alashia. If Alashians are proved to have plundered they shall be punished.

(W. 28 ; S.B.A. xv. 130.)

This letter is important as showing that the Lykian pirates, so well known in later times, were already at their trade in 1500 B.C., and this gives more light on the early Mediterranean shipping, as certainly the rocky coast of Lycia is not the first place to start shipping, and the naval battle, under Ramessu III., at Medinet Habu, is quite in keeping with such pirate habits. The mention of the city of Zikhra may some day be of great value for fixing Alashia; it is not to be found in maps of northern Syria, and if found in Cyprus it would help the identification of the island.

(32) *x* to *y* a fragment naming copper, 30 talents,
procuring much copper for *y*, the land of
Kinakhi. . . .   (W. 31.)

(33) King of ALASHIA to king of Egypt.
Sends his messenger with 500 talents of
copper, apologizes for not sending more in
consequence of pestilence. Asks for silver,
an ox, oil, and one of the " Eagle Conjurers." People quarrel with the king of
A. about his sending wood to Egypt. An
Alashian has died in Egypt, leaving son
and wife at home. Asks for return of
deceased's property by the messenger.
Warns king of E. against kings of Khatti
and of Shankhar, and whatever they send
A., A. will send double to Egypt.

(W. 25 ; S.B.A. xiii. 544.)

(34) Vizier of ALASHIA to Vizier of Egypt;
sends 5 talents of copper and 2 ivory. . . .

(W. 32.)

The above letter of the king seems to
come at the end, when outlying people were
beginning to be disaffected to Egypt by the
quarrel about supplying Egypt with wood.
The reference to "eagle conjurers" is un-
explained ; the words are so read by
different translators, and have been supposed to refer to men who caught eagles
by art, or to men who divined by the

flight of birds, like the Etruscan haruspex. Another indication that trouble was brewing is seen in the ambiguous position of the kings of the Khatti and of Shankhar. The reference to the claim on the property of a merchant who had died is evidence that some principles of international law were recognized, and that the king interfered to obtain justice for private rights. Lastly we see the viziers of the two countries did business together by the messengers; sending small presents, doubtless to receive a return from Egypt.

These letters from Alashia, though not showing the pomp and wealth of Upper Mesopotamia or Babylonia, yet prove the establishment of an organized government, with regular foreign relations, legal rights defined, and an active trade going on. Such is a most interesting view of the early bronze age in Cyprus, and suggests a growth of such institutions during some considerable time before.

15. *Kings of Assyria and Nukhashi.*

Two isolated letters show that other kingdoms also kept up a friendly diplomatic correspondence with Egypt.   From

(35) ASHUR-UBALLITH king of Ashshur to NAPKHURIA. A. received messengers and sent a royal chariot with a pair of horses, two white horses, a chariot without horses, and a seal of blue stone. Asks for gold in return, for a new palace being built. A.'s father Ashur-nadin-akhi sent to Egypt and received 20 talents of gold: king of Khanigalbat sent and had 20 talents of gold. A. asks for as much. The Eg. messengers had been waylaid by the Shuti ; asks for messengers to be quickly returned. (W. 15 ; R.P. xv. 61.)

The other letter shows that Nukhashi had been conquered and made a vassal state by Tahutmes III.

(36) RAMMAN-NIRARI to king of Egypt. R.'s grandfather had been set up over Nukhashi by Manakhbiia (Men-kheper-ra, Tahutmes III.), who anointed him, and established him ; names Takua ; now the king of Khatti is against him ; asks for help.   (W. 37 ; S.B.A. xv. 20.)

As here an established king refers to his grandfather being set up, we must allow about 60 or 70 years to have elapsed. This letter was written at the beginning of the trouble with the Khatti at the close of the reign of Amenhotep III., about 1380 B.C.

So the grandfather was set up about 1440
or 1450 B.C. This throws him decidedly
to the time of Tahutmes III., 1481–1449,
rather than Tahutmes IV., 1423–1414 B.C.
We must read, therefore, Men-kheper-ra,
and not Men-kheperu-ra.

16. *Petty Governors in Peace.*

The remainder of the letters of the peace
are from various governors and chiefs of
smaller states and towns. Some of them
recur again in the troublous times which
followed. But these short letters as a whole
give such a picture of the affairs of the
Egyptian dominions that they should be
read together.

(37) SHUTARNA of Mushikhuna to the king.
　　 Desires some attention, and for a garrison
　　 to occupy the cities.　　　　(W. 232.)

The name of this place does not occur
again, but it was probably in the north, as
the ruler, Shutarna, is named after the king
of Mitani in the preceding generation.

(38) SHUTARNA of　Mushikhuna　to　king:
　　 remainder lost.　　　　　　(W. 233.)

(39) *x* to the king: names the Akhlamu (between
　　 Babylon and Nineveh) and the king of
　　 Karduniash (Babylonia).　　(W. 291.)

(40) *x* to *y*. A king writes to the kings of Kinakhi (Galilee and the Hauran), saying that he is going to send Akia to condole with the king of Egypt. He desires that A. go in safety to the city of Zukhli in Egypt.

(W. 14; B.O.D. 58.)

This condolence must have been on the death of Amenhotep III.; and the issue of this sort of passport points to the country being somewhat disturbed. The city of Zukhli, in Egypt, where the king resided, must be one of the capitals of the country; and remembering the Egyptian union of *l* and *r*, this can hardly be other than the city of Sokari, or now Saqqarah, the main capital Memphis.

(41) MUTZU' . . . to king. King wrote by Khaia about caravans to Khani-galbat, which M. escorted, as (La)paia his father did the caravans to Khani-galbat and Karduniash. Let the king send other caravans and M. will escort them.

(W. 256.)

The restoration of Lapaia is only a guess; and it does not seem very likely, as Lapaia was in Judæa, whereas this writer seems rather to have been in the north. Possibly this . . paia is Yakhzibaia of two other letters (104, 105), of whom no details are known ; or it may be a fresh name.

(42) SHIPTURI ... to the king. Acknowledges letter, guards the city, and provides for caravans.   (W. 242.)

(43) *x* to the king. Names caravans to Buzruna. (Bozrah.)   (W. 145.)

(44) *x* prince of Qanu to king. Ready to join troops.   (W. 251.)

(45) RUSMANIA prince of Taruna to king. Obeisance.   (W. 260.)
      Taruna may be Toran near Tiberias.

(46) ZISHAMINI to king. Obeisance.
                                    (W. 261.)

(47) DASHRU to king. Obeisance.   (W. 245.)

(48) DASHRU to king. Obeisance.   (W. 244.)

(49) GESDINNA to king. Report.
                                    (S.B.A. x. 496.)

(50) SURASHAR prince of . . . .tiashna to king. Obeisance.   (W. 257.)

(51) SHABA . . . . to king. Sends presents.
                                    (W. 222.)

(52) YAB . . . . to SHUMUKHA. . . . Y. is in disgrace.   (W. 223.)

(53) AMAYASHI to king. A. will join troops.
                                    (W. 253.)

(54) YIKTASU to king. Y. guards city.
                                    (W. 254.)

(55) BADUZA to king.   Obedient, and has been
maligned.   (W. 255.)

(56) SHIPTIADDI to king of Egypt.   Acknowledges letter.   Yankhamu is faithful.
(W. 241; B.O.D. 65.)

(57) SHIPTI . . . . to king.   Guards city.
(W. 243.)

(58) ZITRIYARA to king.   Obeisance.
(W. 247.)

(59) ZITRIYARA to king.   Acknowledges letter
and performs orders.   (W. 248; B.O.D. 76.)

(60) ZITRIYARA to king.   Report.
(W. 246; S.B.A. x. 499.)

(61) *x* of Dubu or Gubbu to king, who sent
soldiers to king's army.
(W. 250; B.O.D. 78.)

(62) Fragment naming Ugarit (?)
(W. 287; S.B.A. x. 517.)

(63) SHUBANDI to king.   Obeisance.
(W. 229.)

(64) SHUBANDI to king.   Khanya has come to
S., and S. sends 300 oxen and 30 girls.
(W. 228; S.B.A. xi. 331.)

(65) SHUBANDI to king.   S. was disabled by
illness.   (W. 226; B.O.D. 40.)

(66) SHUBANDI to king, acknowledges letter
and defends his city.   (W. 224; B.O.D. 38.)

(67) SHUBANDI to king, same.
(W. 225; B.O.D. 39.)

(68) SHATIYA to king, guards city of Inishatsi(ri?), and has sent his daughter to the palace for the king.   (W. 249; B.O.D. 77.)

(69) ARTAMANYA of Ziri-bashani (plain of Bashan) to the king, is ready to go with his troops wherever ordered.

(W. 161; R.P. xvii. 99.)

(70) ABDTIRSHI of Khazura to the king. A. guards Khazura, (Hazor, near Tyre).

(W. 203.)

(71) *x* of Khazuri to the king. Will guard the city until the king comes.

(W. 202; B.O.D. 47.)

This city of Khasuri is Hazor, 11 S.E. of Tyre, as shown by letter 183.

(72) PUADDI of Wurza (Yerzeh near Shechem) to king. P. guards his land under Rianapa.

(W. 236; B.O.D. 56.)

(73) PUADDI to king; P. defends his place and is ready to escort caravans.   Names Shakhshikhashikha.   (W. 235; B.O.D. 55.)

(74) PUADDI prince of Wurza to king. Defends city.   (W. 234; S.B.A. xi. 329.)

(75) ARZAWAYA prince of Mikhiza to king. A. will join the troops and send supplies.

(W. 175.)

This Mikhiza appears in another letter as Rukhizi, and was probably on the south side of Hermon, by other references to Arzawaya.

(76) ARZAWAYA to king; acknowledges letter.
(W. 176.)
The following is from a different person, as it refers to the south instead of the north of Palestine.

(77) ARZAYA to king; acknowledges letter, and mentions Gazri (Gezer).   (W. 177.)

(78) ADDUMIKHIR to king.   Obeisance.
(W. 187.)

(79) ADDUMIKHIR to king.   City is secure and obedient.   (W. 188.)

(80) TAGI to king.   Obeisance.   (W. 190.)

(81) TAGI to king.   Sends Takhmaini, and asks for gold.   (W. 265.)

(82) MILKILI to king.   City is safe. . . . Khamu . . . sends to king 6 women, 5 boys, and 5 men.   (W. 168.)
Probably Khamu . . . is Khamuniri.

(83) MILKILI to king.   Acknowledges letter and asks for troops.   (W. 172 ; B.O.D. 63.)

(84) MILKILI to king.   M. will execute an order sent to him.   (W. 169; S.B.A. xi. 371.)

(85) ABDMILKI of Shaskhimi to king.   Ready to join troops.   (W. 252.)

(86) SHUWARDATA to king.   Carries out orders.   (W. 200 ; B.O.D. 69.)

(87) SHUWARDATA to king.   Has sent a present.   (W. 198 ; B.O.D. 67.)

(88) *x* prince of Nazima to king.   States his adhesion.   (W. 263.)

(89) DIYATI to king. Guards city and supplies provision. (W. 264.)

(90) YITIA of Asqaluna (Ashkelon) to king. Guards the city. (W. 210.)

(91) YITIA to king. Y. sends food, drink, oxen, &c., as tribute. (W. 207; B.O.D. 52.)

(92) YITIA to king. Y. supplied the troops with all necessaries. (W. 209; B.O.D. 54.)

(93) YITIA to king. Y. guards city and sends tribute of *Lupakku* stones.
(W. 208; B.O.D. 53.)

(94) YITIA of Asqaluna to king. Guards the city. (W. 211.)

(95) YITIA of Asqaluna to king. Guards the city. (W. 212.)

(96) YITIA to king. Guards the city. The present officer is incapable, and asks that Rianapa be appointed. (W. 213.)

(97) YABNI-ILU prince of Lakisha (Lachish) to king. Obeisance, and attends to message sent by Maia. (W. 218.)

(98) ZIMRIDA prince of Lakisha to king. Has received orders and will execute them.
(W. 217; S.B.A. xiii. 319.)

(99) KHIZIRI to king. Protects Maia according to orders, and provides for troops (see 97).
(W. 259.)

(100) BAIAYA to king. Attends to orders of Maya, and will follow troops. (W. 231.)

(101) YABITIRI of Azzati (Gaza) to king. Yan-
khama took Y. into Egypt when young and
Y. lived in the palace. Y. now guards
Azzati and Yapu (Joppa).

(W. 214; S.B.A. xv. 504.)

(102) ABDNA. . . . to king. Obeisance.

(W. 271.)

(103) INBAUTA to king. Obeisance. (W. 272.)

(104) YAKHZIBAIA to king. Obeisance.

(W. 274.)

(105) YAKHZIBAIA to king. Obeisance.

(W. 266.)

(106) YAMIUTA prince of Ga(?)dashuna to king.
Obeisance.   (W. 267.)

The preceding letters have here been
roughly classed by placing those which
belong to the north first, and then those
of the south. In some cases other clues
help, as the mention of Maia in three letters,
97, 99, 100, connected with Lachish. Other
letters are placed along with those to which
there is a clue by the resemblance of name.
But any strict classification is impossible
with so few data to guide us.

These letters show that frequent reports
were sent to Egypt without there being any
business on hand. The city of Askelon

lying upon the high road had to supply food for the passing troops, and probably Yitia took advantage of a soldier messenger to send in a little report of his providing supplies.

CHAPTER III.

THE NORTH SYRIAN WAR

17. *Trouble in Amki with the Khatti.*

THE next series are the letters which show the gradual breaking up of the state of peace, and the loss of Northern Syria. The troubles seem to have begun in Central Syria, and to have been provoked there by attempts of the Egyptian allies to secure more territory, trusting in their backing from Egypt to support them. In this they were disappointed, and so the power of Egypt first showed its waning by abandoning its friends.

The first four letters refer to attacks on Amki, which by its name (the "hollow" or "deep place") was a large valley, and by its position must have been the upper part of the Litâny river, inland from Beyrut. The chiefs about the lower Litâny, at the bend of the river, thought that they could capture the upper part of the valley.

(107) ILDAYA of Khazi to the king. Warred against cities in the land of Amki, but Idagama of Kinza with the Khatti drove him off. (W. 132.)

(108) BIRI[DASHYA ?] of Khashabu to the king. Warred against cities in the land of Amki, but Idagama of Kinza with the Khatti drove him off. (W. 131.)

(109) *x* (Namiawaza ?) to the king. Warred against cities in the land of Amki, but Idagama of Kinza with the Khatti drove him off. (W. 133 ; B.O.D. 46.)

Here are three letters almost verbally identical from three different chiefs, who had evidently leagued together to attack the upper Litâny valley. The position of the land of Amki is very probably shown by the place 'Ammîk, nineteen miles south-east of Beyrut. The restoration of the name Biridashya is almost certain, as he was acting on Yinuama, and in league with Buzruna and Khalunni in No. 115 ; hence he must have been about the region of Khashabu, the Arabic *Hôshaba*. The result of this affair appears in an extension of Hittite power in the next.

(110) ADDU . . . IA . . . and BATTI - ILU to the king. Khatti and Lupakku have

taken cities of Amki, and cities belonging to A-addu. Zitana and 9 men have arrived in Nukhashi, and writers go to see about them and enquire of king if they really come from him. Greeting to Ben-ili, Abd-urash, Ben-ana, Ben-zidki, Amur-addi, and Anati.   (W. 125 ; R.P. xvii. 99.)

Batti-ilu was a companion of Aziru's brother, as we see in No. 191, and so he probably belonged to Amurri ; as Nukhashi seems to have lain immediately east of the Orontes valley of Amurri this would be very natural.

18. *Trouble about Damascus.*

After this first opening of serious troubles, resulting in the Hittites becoming established in the Litâny valley, the next difficulty is in Aziru coming down from the Orontes valley into the plain of Damascus, and this we learn took place even before the death of Amenhotep III.

(111) AKIZZI to NAM-MUR-IA. A. is governor of Qatna (west of Damascus) ; he has victualled troops, and asks for troops to occupy the country, so as to secure Nukhashi. If they delay in Martu (Amurri, Orontes), Azira will succeed ; and if troops do not march this year he will get the whole

country.   The king of Khatti has burned a city and taken spoils.   Azira has captured men of Qatna, and Akizzi asks for them to be ransomed.   King of Khatti has also taken Shamash, the god of A.'s father, and A. asks for gold to ransom him.

(W. 138; B.O.D. 36.)

(112) AKIZZI to NAM-MUR-IA.   King of Khatti tries to seduce A.   Tiuwatti of Lapana (Helbon), Arzauia of Rukhizi, and Aidagama are leagued; but kings of Nukhashi, Ni, Zinzar, and Kinanat are faithful. Asks for troops soon, as if Arzauia and Tiuwatti come to land of Ubi, and Dasha is in land of Amma, then Ubi will be lost. They daily call on Aidagama to conquer Ubi.   As Timashgi (Damascus) in the land of Ubi stretches out her hands so does Qatna.   (W. 139; B.O.D. 37.)

From this it seems that an alliance of the Hittites in their new possession of the upper Litâny with the neighbouring chiefs, Itakama of the Upper Orontes, and Tiuwatti of the north of Damascus, had been formed to attack the fertile plain of Damascus, which included Qatna.   But several chiefs around this alliance remained faithful.   Another fragment of a letter of Akizzi is

(113) AKIZZI to the king. Complains of delay, and names Kinza the city of Itakama.
(W. 140.)

19. *Namyawaza in Trouble.*

The other side of the matter appears in a letter from Itakama, complaining of the forward movement of the Egyptian party, which we noticed in letters 107–109. Very possibly letter 109, of which the writer's name is lost, was from Namyawaza.

(114) ITAKAMA to the king. Namyawaza has maligned him, and occupied all the land of I.'s father in the land of Gidshi (Qedesh by Lake Homs). I. appealed to Pukhari the deputy. N. has delivered all the cities in the land of Gidshi and in Ubi (Upper Orontes and Damascus plain) to the Khabiri. I. offers to drive out the Khabiri and N. (W. 146.)

The politics are complex, as there appears to have been a triangular duel going on, owing to everybody fighting for their own hand. Itakama was opposed to Namyawaza (see 114); Namyawaza was opposed to Biridashyi (see 116, 117); and we can hardly doubt that Biri . . . is Biridashyi opposed to Idagama (see 108). Namyawaza was certainly on the Egyptian side, as he was supported by the Egyptian resident, who reckoned Biridashya as an enemy (see 122). The best way to understand this seems to be that at first Namyawaza was pro-Egyptian, and Itakama and Biridashyi neutral. Then owing to the aggression of N. and B. upon I., I. was thrown into opposition and was successful (108, 109). Finding I. successful, B. changed sides and attacked N. with I. as we see in 116.

The Egyptian ally, Namyawaza, sends his own version in a very full historical letter (116), which we here preface by a note (115), which shows how the Khabiri and Sati were originally allies of the Egyptians.

(115) NAMYAWAZA to the king. Reports his readiness for service with his soldiers, chariots, brothers, his Khabiri, and his Suti. (W. 144 ; R. P. xvii. 96.)

This letter is important as showing that the SAGAS, who are generally taken as the same as the Khabiri, were at their earliest appearance—while yet allies of the Egyptian party—employed in Central Syria, and were thus beyond the limits of the subsequent occupation of Palestine by the Hebrews. This should suffice to show how futile is any connection proposed between the SAGAS, Khabiri, and the Hebrew invasion, which by all accounts took place in the south of Palestine. We must regard the SAGAS, Khabiri, or "confederates," as an alliance of Syrian tribes near Damascus; though it is possible that Hebron took its name from that alliance when its conquests had spread to the south. The Khabiri are mentioned by name only in the letters of Abd-khiba.

(116) [NAMYAWAZA] to the king. Biridashya has made the city of Yinuama rebel, and brought chariots to the city of Ashtarti, and delivered it to the Khabiri. Kings of Butsruna and Khalunni join with Biridashya, and say, "Come on, we will kill Namyawaza." So N. took refuge in . . . . . (? Dimashqa.) N. claimed to be an Egyptian subject, and Artsawaya went to Gizza, brought Azira's troops, took Shaddu, and gave it to the Khabiri. Itakama has destroyed Gizza, and Artsawaya and Biridashya will destroy Abitu. N. will defend Kumidi. (W. 142; B.O.D. 43.)

(117) NAMIAWAZA to king. Asks for troops, and that Biridashya and Bawanamash be punished by the king. (W. 143.)

F

The history of this fighting is obvious, with the map in hand. Itakama having repelled the Egyptian advance under Namyawaza, Biridashya turned and sided with the winning side. He attacked the land behind Tyre, at Yinuama (*Yanuh*), and fearing that Namyawaza would come down the Litâny and fight him at Khashabu (*Hôshaba*), or Yinuama, he crossed over eastward and drew the chiefs of Khalunni (Gaulonitis, *Jaulan*) and Butsruna (Bozrah) to attack Namyawaza on the east, driving him to take care of himself and take refuge, perhaps, in Damascus ; but, unhappily, some words are missing at this part. Then Arzawaya and Itakama were at leisure, with Biridashya, to ravage northern Galilee, taking or threatening Gizza (*Gish*), Shaddu (*Shatiyeh*), and Abitu (*Abdeh*). But Namyawaza succeeded so far in holding the important post of Kumidi (*Kamid*), in the Litâny valley on the road from Damascus to Beyrut.

20. *Galilee Rebelling.*

The next letter shows the rebellion spreading just south of this region, in southern Galilee. From the names of places of which news is sent, this letter must have

been written from some place near Akka;
and as it was a safe place, in communication
with Egyptians, it was probably from Akka
itself, but we know nothing more of
Mutaddi.

(118) MUTADDI to YANKHAMU. Aiab has
fled, also the king of Bikhishi, before the
Egyptian officer. Bininima, Tadua, and
Yashuia are there. *x* was driven out of
Ashtarti. Cities of the land of Gar (Gur)
rebel, Udumu (Adamah), Aduri (*Et Tireh*),
Araru (*Arareh*), Mishtu (*Mushtah*), Magdali,
(Magdala), and Khinianabi ('*Anân ?*). Also,
Tsarqi, Khawini (*Kâaûn*), and Yabishi
(Yabesh) are taken. *Y* came to Bikhishi
and heard the Egyptian orders. (W. 237.)

This land of Gar is the Heb. Gur,
and seems from the places named to have
included all the southern half of Galilee.
Thus at this point we find that all Galilee
was lost to the Egyptians. Further news
comes from Akka.

(119) SURATA, of Akka, to the king. Obeisance.
(W. 157.)
Sharatu was father of Shutatna, as we see
in letter 124.

(120) ZATATNA, of Akka, to the king.
Obeisance. (W. 158.)

(121)   ZITATNA, of Akka, to the king.
Obeisance.   (W. 160; B.O.D. 32.)

(122)   ZATATNA, of Akka, to the king.
[Ziri]dayashda [? Biridashya] fled from
Namyawaza . . . . . Shuta, the (Egyptian)
officer. Egyptian soldiers are in Makida
with a female. Shuta sent to Zatatna
ordering Z. to deliver Zirdayashda to
Namyawaza, but it was impossible to do
so. Akka is like Magdali in Egypt, let
it not be taken by these men.
          (W. 159; R.P. xvii. 95.)

This last letter seems as if it might well
refer to Biridashya, who had suffered a
reverse from Namyawaza, and fled to the
Egyptians in Akka; we know nothing
else of Zirdayashda, and the resemblance to
the name Biridashya is near enough to be
thought of in connection with well-known
bungles of the scribes and uncertainties of
modern reading.

(123)   AKIZZI to the king. Refers to a caravan (?) in the third year; names Bidinaza.
          (W. 290.)

This letter must have been written after
the death of Amenhotep III., as otherwise
the third year (of Amenhotep IV.) would
not be named; so it must be subsequent to

the other letters of Akizzi, 111, 112. The difficulty about caravans seems to have been felt now that Galilee was in rebellion, thus cutting the road to northern Syria and Mesopotamia. The last letter of Burnaburyash refers to this matter.

(124) BURNABURYASH to NAPKHURU-RIA. B.'s merchants went with Akhithabu, and stayed in Kinakhi (E. of Merom) on business; Akhithabu went on, and then in the city of Khinatuni (Kanawat) in Kinakhi, Shumadda (of Merom, see 125), son of Balumi, and Shutatna, son of Sharatu of Akkaiu, killed them and took the caravan. As Kinakhi belongs to Egypt, so Napkhururia must subdue these robbers and compensate the owners of the goods, otherwise trade will be cut off. Shumadda has kept one of the Babylonians with his feet cut off. Shutatna has taken another as his slave. These must be returned. Present sent 1 maneh of enamel (?). Desires messenger to be returned soon.

(W. 11 ; R.P. xv. 65.)

Who Shumadda was is shown by the following short note, written probably earlier, while he was allied to Egypt.

(125) SHAMUADDU, prince of Shamkhuna, to the king. Has received message.

(W. 220 ; S.B.A. xii. 328.)

Another letter seems to belong to the rebellious times, excusing not giving tribute.

(126) SHUMADDU to the king. S. does not send soon because his father, Kuzuna, did not do so. (W. 221; B.O.D. 66.)

The position of Shummada at Shamkhuna, allied with Akka, and attacking Kanawat, is clearly identified with the name of Lake Merom in Greek times, Semekhonitis. This seems derived from some district named Semkhon by the Lake, probably the region of the spring of *Semakh*, six miles to the north-east of the lake. The history of this plundering of the caravans is very clear, and shows that Galilee was more rebellious than the Hauran at that time. The names are some of them familiar in the Jewish writings of a later time, as Ahitub (Akhi-thabu), Shema-yah (parallel to Shamu-Addu), and Balumi (Balaam).

21. *Aziru in Peace.*

We now turn to the more northern part of Syria where the rebellion of Aziru, which we saw beginning in Akizzi's letter (111), was steadily successful until he became paramount in all that region. We begin a little before that letter of Akizzi (111) in order to show the earlier position of Aziru, the most energetic son of Abd-ashratu, lord of Amurri, or the middle Orontes valley.

(127) ABDASHT[AR]TI to king.   Obeisance.
(W. 40; B.O.D. 34.)

(128) AZIRI to king.   Sends two men as slaves (? messengers) and asks for their return to Amurri.   (W. 42; S.B.A. xv. 21.)

(129) . . . KHIBIYA to resident.   Obeisance. Guards city, but enmity is powerful. A message has come from Amurri.   (W. 258.)

The above seem to show Aziru as an obedient subject.   But he soon falls under suspicion and seeks to excuse himself.

(130) AZIRI to DUDU (Egyptian resident).   A. has done all that the king desired, and rules the land of Amuri.   Desires D. to vindicate him from certain slanders.
(W. 44; S.B.A. xiii. 217.)

(131) [ABDASHRATU ?] to DUDU.   Asks for the return of Aziru back quickly from Egypt.   The kings of Nukhashi said to A. that his father sent gold to the king of Egypt but got nothing in return.   Refers to his Suti troops.
(W. 52; S.B.A. xiii. 216.)

From this it seems that Aziru was in Egypt as a hostage or messenger, and his father was pointing out his fidelity in order to get his son back again. The great opponent of Aziru's advance was Ribaddi, the governor of northern Phoenicia, and the series of his letters is the most important of all. We turn back a little here to take up his earlier notes before the great struggle.

(132) [AMANAPPA ?] to RIBADDU. R. had reported a plague in Tsumuri among people and sheep. A. orders him to send sheep, which are the king's. (W. 89.)

(133) *x* to *y*. Mentions Ribaddi, Abdaddi, and Benazi. (W. 116.)

(134) RIBADDI to the king. Names the Khabiri and the officer Amanappa. . . . Let Yapa-addi be blamed. . . . Two of R.'s ships have been seized by Yapa-addi (?).
(W. 106; S.B.A. xi. 361.)

Other chiefs were also finding difficulties overtaking them about this time.

(135) YAMA to the king. Y. defends his cities till help shall come.
(W. 238; S.B.A. xi. 392.)

(136) SHUBANDU to the king. The Khabiri are strong. (W. 227.)

(137) SUBAYADI to the king. Towns captured. S. is unable to defend his. Asks for troops. Khazu is against him.   (W. 268.)

(138) ILKHA . . . to the king. The governors are destroyed, and all land falls away to Khabiri. Asks for Suti troops.

(W. 283 ; B.O.D. 80.)

We now turn back to Ribaddi beginning his determined struggle against Aziru.

(139) RIBADDI to the king. R. will defend the king's city. R.'s gifts which are with Yapa-addu Y. will show the king.

(W. 72.)

(140) RIBADDI to the king. Asks for troops to defend the king's land from Abdashirta and the Khabiri.   (W. 73.)

(141) RIBADDI to the king. King promised to send Iribaiasha, who has not come. The Khabiri surround R.   (W. 99.)

(142) RIBADDI to AMANAPPA (Egyptian resident). R. asked A. to deliver him from Abdashirta and the Khabiri. R. was ordered to send a ship to Yarimuta ; asks for soldiers to occupy Amurri.

(W. 59 ; M.A.F. vi. 307 ; R.P. xviii. 62.)

22. *Abdashirta stating his fidelity.*

But Abdashirta was not at all ready to be classed as an enemy of Egypt.

(143) ABDASHRAT to the king. A. declares
that his enemies are strong, and desires
protection; will obey all commands, and
sends ten women. (W. 39; B.O.D. 33.)

(144) The end of a letter apparently from ABDA-
SHIRTA to the king. Khaya is hostile to
the king. Let not the ships of Ziduna and
Biruta come to Amurri to kill Abdashirta.
Let the king seize the ships of Arwada
which are in Egypt, and which were left
by Mani with A. A. asks for a governor
to be put in Ziduna and Biruta, who will
supply him with a ship, or else the Amurri
will kill him. (W. 124; B.O.D. 44.)

Here we see Abdashirta striving to make
out that he was in danger owing to his
friendship for Egypt, and abusing Khaya
who was the regular Egyptian agent or
officer. The request for a new governor
in Zidon and Berut is evidently to super-
sede Ribaddi, who was sincerely in Egyptian
interest, and against Abdashirta. Or, possibly, Ribaddi was not yet in charge of
those cities, as we find a Zimrida governor
of Zidon.

(145) ZIMRIDI to king. Z. is prince of Ziduna,
which is safe; but all his other cities
have fallen to the Khabiri, and he asks
for troops and succour.

(W. 147; S.B.A. xiii. 318.)

(146) ZIMRIDI to the king. Mentions Zumuri
    being in Egyptian hands.   (W. 148.)

All the subterfuges of Abdashirta would
not suffice to stifle the complaints against
him, and a long and severe letter was sent
to him from Egypt, of which fortunately a
copy is preserved.

(147) The king to the Chief of Amurra. The
    Chief of Gubla (Ribaddi?), living in
    Zituna, asked the Chief of Amurra to
    help him, but was not protected. Amurra
    has allied with the Chief of Qidsha
    (Itakama?), who is an enemy. The king
    does not wish to threaten the land of
    Kinakhi; and asks A. to send his son to
    Egypt as a hostage, and allows this year
    for him to do so; next year will be too
    late. A. had asked for Khanni in place
    of the king, to deliver to him the enemies.
    A. is asked to help in bringing in Sharru
    and all his sons, Tuya, Liya and all his
    sons, Yishiari and his sons, the son-in-law
    of Malia and his sons and wives . . . .
    Dashirti, Paluma, and Nimmakhi the
    Khapadu in Amurri.
                  (W. 50; S.B.A. xiii. 224.)

Here we have the official Egyptian rebuke
for the alliance of which we saw the effects
in letters 107-109. And about this time we,

have Aziri's letters excusing his going into Egypt as a hostage, in compliance with the Egyptian demand. The first refers probably to the bearer of the previous letter.

(148) AZIRI to DUDU. Khatib has come from the king; the king of Khatti has come into Nukhashi, and therefore Aziri and Khatib must stay.

(W. 45 ; S.B.A. xiii. 229.)

(149) AZIRI to KHAI. A. and Khatib will soon leave. King of Khatti is in Nukhashi, and A. guards the land of Martu (= Amurra), and fears the fall of the city of Dunip.

(W. 46; S.B.A. xiii. 231.)

(150) AZIRI to the king. A. and Paluia serve the king. A. and Khatib will come soon, but the king of Khatti is in Nukhashi; there are two roads to Tunip, and A. fears its fall. (W. 47; S.B.A. xiii. 232.)

The successes of the Khatti, pushing south to the land of Hamath, in real agreement with Aziri, as we see by letter 111, are skilfully used as a reason for his remaining where he was, and not leaving for Egypt. The fact of Tunip not being yet in the hands of the Khatti, while it seems to lie on the highway to Nukhashi, may point to one of the following conclusions : (1) The advance of the Khatti had been to the Euphrates first, then down the stream and striking across by the Sebkha to the Orontes Valley, thus cutting off Tunip ; or (2) Tunip may have been in Aziru's hands, in real alliance with the Khatti, though he professes to fear them ; or (3) Nukhashi must be placed as far north as Tunip. Of these the first seems the probable truth.

23. *Ribaddi attacked.*

We next enter on the long series of Ribaddi's letters.

(151) RIBADDI to king.   Abd-ashrat holds R.'s cities, and was not ashamed at R.'s complaint.   King wrote to king of Biruna and king of Tsiduna. . . .   (W. 58.)

(152) RIBADDI to king.   R. cannot send ships to Zalukhi and Ugarit because of Aziru. The Khatti are plundering the lieges of Gubla.   (W. 104.)

(153) RIBADDI to king.   Names city of Tisa . . . in land of Tsumuri, and land of Martu (Amurri).   (P.A. 35 No. 3.)

(154) RIBADDI to the king.   Names Tsumuri and Abdashirta.   (P.A. 35 No. 2.)

These letters belong to the beginning of the troubles, and it cannot be settled exactly where they were written.   The sending of ships to Ugarit shows that it was on the coast, and not far inland as has been proposed. As we have already noticed, the mouth of the Orontes appears to be the place ; and Ugarit or Akaritu seems to be the Okrad or Akrad—Kurdland—of modern times. Zalukhi must also be on the coast.

(155) RIBADDI to the king.   R. is only friendly with Tsumura.   Sent two messengers to the king, but not returned.   Asks for general to come and take Abdashirta and Aziru.   Ullaza named.   If troops not sent land will fall to the Khabiri; or at least write to Yankhamu or Bikhura to occupy Amurru.   R. strives with Yapa-addu and Khatib.   Asks for troops and people of Milukha to save the city from falling to the Khabiri.   (W. 75 ; R.P. xviii. 52.)

(156) RIBADDI, governor of Gubla, to the king. Tsumur is not taken, but in great danger. Yapa-addi afflicts R.   Abdashirta's sons are tools of the kings of Mitani, Kash, and the Khatti.   Let troops be sent with Yankhamu .... Yarimuta .... deputy of Kumidi (*i.e.* Bikhura). . . .

(W. 87 ; R.P. xviii. 59.)

This last letter was evidently written from Gubla; and so, therefore, probably also was the letter before it. It appears that Ribaddi was chief of Gubla, and in more or less authority over all northern Phoenicia, as he stays to and fro in various cities during his troubles. The next letter was probably also written from Gubla.

(157) RIBADDI to king. Enquiries about R.'s messenger, who had been despoiled; Khabiri takes possession of all lands. If R. agrees with Abd-ashirta as Yapa-addi and Zimrida did he would be safe. If Tsumur is lost, and Bit (Su?) arti is given to Yankhamu, he ought to give corn to R. Shuti people are against R. Tell Y. that R. is really the king's. R. has written to Y. that if Y. will not help, R. must abandon city. Names Milkuru and Mutshi (?). (W. 61.)

This shows that Zidon was now lost, as we know that Zimrida was governor of that city (145), and in all later letters we shall see that Zidon belongs to the enemy.

24. *Ribaddi in Simyra.*

(158) RIBADDI to king. R. is distressed by sons of Abdashirta who occupy Amurri. Only Tsumura and Irqata are left, and R. is in Tsumura, for the deputy fled from Gubla . . . Zimrida . . . and Yapaaddu . . . against R., and would not attend to deputy. Ask for troops for Tsumura and Irqata, those of Tsumura having fled.

(W. 78; R.P. xv. 70.)

This last letter shows Ribaddi to have moved from Gubla to Tsumura in order to maintain its defence, the troops having deserted. The city of Irqata appealed also directly to Egypt; and this and the letter of the men of Tunip are interesting pieces of evidence of a municipal government then, which could conduct public affairs in its own name, without being headed by an individual. It begins "Irqata and its elders fall down at the feet of the king."

(159) IRQATA, city, to the king. Babikha was sent by the king. People in land of Shanku are enemies. Strong appeal for help. (W. 122; B.O.D. 42.)

It may be this [Ba?]bikha is the same as Abbikha of one of the last letters, who was then rebellious.

(160) *x* [Ribaddi ?] to the king.   Names Abdashirti,
and people of Shikhlali.   *x* has been driven
out of Irqata, and is in Tsumuri.   He
delivered Shabi-ilu, Bishitanu, Maia, and
Arzaya from the people of Shikhlali, and
they are staying at the palace.   Names
Yabaia.   (W. 126.)

This letter was written from Tsumura,
and yet after the fall of Irqata, so it must
belong to this position as there is no sign of
Ribaddi being later at Tsumura.

25. *Ribaddi in Gubla.*

The next thirteen letters of Ribaddi are
from Gubla.

(161) RIBADDI to king.   May the goddess of
Gubla give power to the king.   Aziru is
his enemy, has taken 12 of R.'s men, and
asks 50 of silver ransom.   A. has taken
in Yibuliya men whom R. had sent to
Tsumura.   Ships of Tsumura, Biruta, and
Ziduna all gone over to land of Amurri
(*i.e.*, to Aziri).   Yapa-addi as well as Aziri
attacks R., and have taken one of his ships,
and sail out on the sea to capture his
others.   R.'s subjects will go over to enemy
if not succoured.   R. holds Tsumura, but
is surrounded by enemies.   Asks Amanma
if R. did not accompany him to Alashia on

G

his way to Egypt.   R. asks for help to get
food from Yarimuta.   Yapa-addi would not
let Amanma go to Alashia, and is joined
with Aziri.   (S.B.A. xv. 359.)

This is the first mention of getting food
for Gubla from Yarimuta ; two earlier letters
name Yarimuta (142, 156), but its real
importance to Gubla comes out during the
siege and famine.   It was obviously near to
Gubla, and a prosperous city in a fertile
country, as it exported provision.   It was
probably to the north of Gubla, as all the
places to the south are referred to by
Ribaddi as being in his charge, whereas
Yarimuta was beyond his scope.   All this
agrees to the position of the next important
place north of Gubla, now *Latakia* —
Laodicea—at the mouth of a large river,
the *Nahr el Kebir*.   Yarimuta is obviously
a Yerimoth, or Ramoth = a "high place";
and the pre-Greek name of Laodicea was
Ramitha, which exactly agrees to this.   The
importance of shipping on this coast should
be observed ; there were sea-fights, when
vessels put out on the high seas to intercept
and capture others.   The reference to going
to Alashia on the way to Egypt is somewhat
puzzling, as Cyprus is off the line that we

should expect for shipping between Gubla and Egypt. Yet it is a valuable allusion in two ways; (1) it shows that Gubla could not be at Byblos as is often supposed, as that would be much farther from any possible site for Alashia; and (2) it almost shows that Alashia cannot be on the Syrian coast from the Orontes northward, as that would be an impossible position to take on the way to Egypt. It was possible to go across to Cyprus in order to get the larger and better shipping which seems to have. regularly traded to Egypt with copper (see 28, 29); but any position further up the coast would be impossible in this view.

(162) RIBADDI to king. Bumabula (?) son of Abdasherta holds Ullaza, Ardata, Yikhliya, Ambi, and Shigata; R. asks for help to Tsumura, for A.'s sons conquer the king's land for the kings of Mitani and Kash. If king waits till they take Tsumura, what will become of R? who cannot go to help Tsumura. Ambi, Shigata, Ullaza, and Yada revolt, and R. fears that Gubla will fall into hands of Khabiri.

(W. 86; R.P. xviii. 58.)

Here we find that the rebels had seized most of the coast, and only the more important places were holding out against them.   Ullaza (*El Usy*), Ardata (*Arthûsi*), Shigata (*Sukât*), and Tsumura (*Sumra*), are all pretty certainly known ; and they help us to gain some idea of the position of Yikhliya, which agrees well to *Qleiät* between Tsumura and Ardata ; and Ambi, which is often named with Shigata, and was probably near it, may well be *Baldeh*, an ancient port lying next to *Sukât*.   We have seen before (letter 156) that the kings of Mitani and Kash were said to be behind all this trouble, and pushing on Aziri to act for them.   Of the king of Mitani this may well be believed so far as position goes.   But Kash is usually supposed to be Babylonia, yet such an accusation against a distant land is unlikely.   It is repeated in 172.   In 193 we see 600 men of Kashi asked for to defend Gubla, and in 214 such a request is repeated.   In 234 Naharain and Kash are linked together as being both within reach of the Egyptian ships, and in 254 the Kashi are interfering in the south by Jerusalem. All these references show that Babylonians cannot be thought of in such connections ; and we must rather look to the region of Mitani and Naharain, bordering on Amurra, and on or close to the sea. Possibly the name may remain in Mount Kasios, which belonged to the land of the warlike Kurds, the Akarit or Ugarit.

(163) RIBADDI to the king. R. fears that Tsumura will fall to the Khabiri. Pakhamnata was in Tsumura and supplied Gubla with food, and after that ordered it from Yarimuta. (W. 88.)

(164) RIBADDI to the king. Abd-ashirta is camping against Tsumura. Gubla as well as Khikubta belong to the king. Send back Abd-Ninib, whom R. sent with Bukhiya.
(W. 53.)

The mention of ordering food from Yarimuta to Gubla, after Tsumura could not supply it, shows that Yarimuta must have been a very near port to Gubla, and agrees with its being Ramitha. The place Khikubta, which is said to belong to the king, is supposed to be Ha-ka-ptah, Memphis; and so the sense would be that Gubla is as much the king's as his own capital. This seems very probable.

(165) RIBADDI to king. Tsumura is like a bird in a snare, let the king look to it. Sons of Abdashirta on land and Arwada by sea . . . sent . . . to Yankhami. . . . If ships come

from Eg. they will not fear Abdashirta.   A.
has seized Ullaza.   R. is not strong enough
to aid Tsumura, for Yapa-addu is contrary,
and has plundered R., who complained to
Amanappa and Turbikhaza and Yankhami.
No grain left.   (W. 84.)

(166) RIBADDI to king.   Asks for men from
Misri and Milukha and horses.   Has sold
everything to Yarimuta for food.   King
ordered Khaya to be brought to Tsumur;
R. gave 13 of silver and garments to the
Khabiri when he brought letter to Tsumur.
Khaya is there, ask him.   (W. 74.)

This request for troops shows that Milukha must be an ally of Egypt, and the
men of Milukha like the Shardani in the
Egyptian service.   As they are most likely
Syrians, we should find Milukha probably
on the Syrian coast; and it seems very
likely that these men (also asked for in 155
and 175) were the mainlanders of Tyre, for
close south-east of Tyre is *Khurbet el
Meluhiyeh.*   The Tyrians would naturally
have a body of trained troops to defend
Tyre, and such seem to have been taken
as organized auxiliaries into the Egyptian
service.   As, however, *Milukha* means

merely "saltness," it might be applied to more than one place.

(167) RIBADDI to king.   Let Buribita stay in Tsumura, and let Khaib take message, and appoint him over feudal princes.   Aziru and his brothers before Gubla.   Thus Tsumura cannot hold out.   No silver to buy horses, all spent for food. (W. 80.)

(168) [RIBADDI to the king.]   Aziru attacks Gubla (?).   Tsumura is in danger.
(W. 95.)

(169) RIBADDI to the king.   Formerly Mitani was hostile to the king's fathers, but R. was always faithful to his fathers.   Names Yankhamu . . . and land of Subari ; . . . kings of Kinaakhni used to flee from the Egyptians, but now Abdashirta's sons resist.   R. cannot lead an officer into Tsumura.   All R.'s cities have fallen away. If Khaib and Amanappa have Tsumura . . .
(W. 101.)

These letters deal with the danger of Simyra, which seems to have lasted for some time, as eight letters (162–169) are written in nearly the same terms about it.   The fall of Tsumur was a main event in the history of the war ; but before we proceed to that we should notice some other letters that seem to

come in during this rise of the power of
Aziru, resuming the history of Tsumur
at 172.

(170) People of DUNIP to the king. Who would
      formerly have plundered Dunip without
      being plundered by Manakhbiria? The
      gods of Egypt dwell in Dunip. But we
      now belong no more to Egypt. For 20
      years (on times) we have sent messengers,
      but they remain with the king; now we
      desire the return of Yadi-addu, who had
      been given by the king and then ordered to
      return to him. Azira has captured people
      in the land of Khatat. A. will treat Dunip
      as he has treated Nii; and if we mourn the
      king will also have to mourn. And when
      Azira enters Tsumuri he will do to us as he
      pleases, and the king will have to lament.
      "And now Dunip your city weeps, and her
      tears are running, and there is no help for
      us. For 20 years we have been sending to
      our lord, the king, the king of Egypt, but
      there has not come to us a word from our
      lord, not one."   (W. 41 ; S.B.A. xv. 18.)

This touching end to the letter is probably
a picture of much of the state of Syria at
this time, gradually forced by hard necessity
and neglect to give up an alliance which had
become a real bond of loyalty during the

easy yoke of the great kings of the previous generations. This letter is of the greatest interest, together with the previous one from the elders of Irqata (159), as showing that municipal rule was readily adopted, without even any official head being elected. These cities seem to have been republics, like the Greek cities under Roman rule, managing their own affairs subject to a suzerain, and sending embassies and conducting political business by their council of elders. The date of this letter is shown to be before the fall of Tsumura, yet after the fall of Ni, which still was safe in letter 112, and after the rise of Azira into command, and his bringing Tsumura into danger.

(171) YAPAKHI-ADDI to YANKHAMI. Why does Yan. neglect Tsumura? All is falling to Aziru from Gubla to Ugarit. Shigata and Ambi are revolting. Ships before (?) Ambi and Shigata, and we cannot enter Tsumura.   (W. 123.)

This letter again belongs to the time of the extremity of Tsumura, when it was closely besieged.

26. *Simyra lost.*

Henceforward Tsumura belongs to the enemy, and one great landmark in the history is passed.

(172) RIBADDI to the king.   Abdashirta is strong against R., and sends to Mitana and Kash.   A. has collected the Khabiri against Shigata and Ambi.   "Tsumura, your fortress is now in the power of the Khabiri."

(W. 56; R.P. xviii. 56.)

(173) AZIRI to the king.   A. has carried out all his orders.   The kings of Nukhashi are hostile, and therefore A. has not built up the city of Tsumuri, but will do so within a year.   (W. 48; S.B.A. xi. 410.)

Here Aziri is playing the faithful subject, and excusing his wasting the city of Simyra by the plea that he is so much occupied in resisting the kings of Nukhashi. That Tsumur was left waste after being taken, is seen by the next letter of Ribaddi's.

(174) RIBADDI to king.   Tsumura has fallen, but is not occupied by enemy.   War against R. now for five years . . . Yapakhi-addi . . . . Zimrida (of Sidon) and princes are

against R. and Tsumura. Asks to have
Yankhamu sent, and for 20 pair of horses.

(W. 85.)

(175) RIBADDI to the king. The sons of
Abdashirta have taken horses and chariots
and have delivered men to the land of
Suri. When R. wrote to the king's father
he listened and sent troops to resist A.
When R. sent lately two messengers to
Tsumura, the deputy prevented a message
going to the king. Messengers now have
to go to and fro by night because of the
"Dog" (Abdashirta). If R. is distrusted
let him retire, and let the King send and
drive the Khabiri out of Tsumura. R. asks
for 20 men of Milukha and 20 from Egypt
to defend the city.

(W. 83; R.P. xviii. 50.)

This shows that Ribaddi was correspond-
ing with Amenhotep III., and already had
trouble with Azira at that time, which is in
accord with the time of Azira's rise, in letter
111. A stray ruler, otherwise unknown, may
be noticed here.

(176) NURTUYA . . . . MA to the king.
Defends his city, which is about to fall,
and his father is slain.   (W. 262.)

27. *Abimilki of Tyre in trouble.*

Tyre next claims our notice, as it fell shortly after Tsumura. The letters about it are here grouped together, but probably the first eight should be interspersed somewhat between the defection of Zimrida after letter 145, and, perhaps, the fall of Tsumura, in letter 172. Certainly letter 185 is after letter 172.

(177) ABIMILKI to the king. A. addresses the king at great length and very effusively. A. guards the city of Tsurri until troops come to give him water to drink and wood to burn. Zimrida, of Ziduna, daily has news about Egypt from the rebel Aziri, Abdasharta's son. (W. 149; S.B.A. xv. 518.)

(178) ABIMILKI to the king. A. cannot leave his city to see the king because of Zimrida, of Ziduna, who will attack him if he leaves. Asks for 20 men to guard the city in his absence. Is hemmed in without water or wood. Sent Ilu-milki with 5 talents of copper and other gifts. King asked for news from Kinakhna. The king of Danuna is dead; his brother rules in peace. City of Ugarit is half burnt. The Khatti are quiet. Itakama took Qedesh, and Aziru has begun to fight Namyawaza. Zimrida has collected ships from Aziri's city against Abimilki.

(W. 151; S.B.A. xv. 507.)

The city of Danuna named here is *Danian*, the Hebrew Danyaan, at the Tyrian Steps, on the headland south of Tyre. The references to Itakama and Aziru fighting Namyawaza, are later than the attack by Namyawaza upon Itakama, but show that this letter probably goes in somewhere before the present point. The allusions to Zimrida, however, put it after letter 145 ; and that in its turn cannot be put earlier, as then the Khabiri had already taken all the region of Sidon.

The request for twenty men is like the modern idiom of Egypt in asking for two piastres, as a modest way of applying for an indefinite amount. The position of Tyre, on an island, has always made the supply of wood and of water a difficulty in war.

(179) ABIMILKI to the king.   King gave orders to supply grain and water, but it has not been done.   A. is the servant of Shalma-yati, and Tsurri is the city of Shalmayati. Names Tsumuri.   Prince of Ziduna (Zim-rida) has come with two ships, and A. will go with all his ships.

(W. 152 ; S.B.A. xv. 515.)

(180) ABIMILKI to the king.   A. will defend
city, and come to see the king.   Asks for
Usu for his life (*i.e.*, Hosah, to supply
water).   (W. 153.)

(181) ABIMILKI to the king.   *x* and Zimrida
fight him.   (W. 155.)

(182) ABIMILKI to the king.   Since the troops
left the prince of Zidon (Zimrida) stops his
getting wood and water.
                         (W. 156; S.B.A. x. 498.)

All of these letters must be about the
same period.   Shalmayati seems to be the
god of Tyre.

(183) ABI MILKI to the king.   A. asks for Uzu
to supply food and water.   The prince of
Ziduna takes away his people, and therefore
he asks for Uzu.   Princes of Ziduna and of
Khazura have joined the Khabiri.   Let the
king enquire of his officer in Kinakhi.
                         (W. 154; S.B.A. xiii. 323.)

This Khazura was Hazor, 11 S.E. of
Tyre, which prince had earlier reported his
allegiance, in letters 70, 71.

(184) ABIMILKI to the king.   King set A. in
Tsurri.   A. asks for 20 soldiers to defend
the city, so that he may come to Egypt.
Names Aziru Abdashrat's son [A. ?] khuni-
milki, Khabi, . . .   Tsumura lost to Azira.

Zimrida has seized Uzu, after the troops abandoned it, and there is no water, and no wood, nor burial ground.   Zimrida of Ziduna and Azira rebel, allied with people of Arwada, and collect ships, chariots, and soldiers to seize Tsurri, and they have taken Tsumura.

(W. 150; S.B.A. xv. 511.)

This ends the correspondence of Abi-milki, who seems to have found the force of circumstances too strong for him, as Ribaddi next reports his defection.

28. *Ribaddi in Beyrut.*

(185) RIBADDI to the king.   Tsurri is rebelling under Ya milki (?).   R.'s property was put into Tsurri with R.'s sister and her sons, who have been killed with the commander; the sister's daughters were sent there to be safe from Abdashirta.   Tsurri is not like the land of a feudal prince, but is as Ugarita.   (W. 70; R.P xviii. 63.)

(186) RIBADDI to the king.   Names city of Yabu (?).   R. was not in Biruna.   Aziru has taken Tsumuri.   If abandoned by the king, all will fall to Aziri.   *x* came to Biruna to negotiate with Khamunira. Half the city is attached to Abdashirta's sons and half to the king.   When R. came

to Biruna he sent his son to the king, but for three months he has not seen the king. R. sent a man as far as Takhida, but he was seized. Names land of Yabu. A city will say Ribaddi remains in Biruna, no one comes to the rescue, and they will join Aziri. Gublites write asking if troops will be soon sent. Asks for troops that sons of Abdashirta may not take Biruna. (W. 91.)

The land of Yabu, or Yapu, is unknown, unless it be Yapu—Joppa—down in the south, which seems unlikely. It seems that Ribaddi tried to attract help by sending his son to personally represent the case in Egypt, but quite fruitlessly. Takhida is unknown, and no such name exists on the road to Egypt. After Ribaddu went to Beyrut, his brother Rabimur ruled at Gubla in his absence.

(187) RABIMUR to the king. R. prays the king not to neglect Gubla. Aziru has killed kings of Ammia, Ardata, and Ni, . . . R. begs for 30 or 50 men for Gubla. Messages from Tsumuru and a governor now killed, show that Aziru is a rebel.

(W. 120; B.O.D. 45.)

(188) RABIMUR to the king. Aziru killed Aduna king of Irqata, king of Ammia,

King of Ardata, and the deputy. Also
has Tsumura and other cities. Gubla alone
remains . . . Ullaza . . . Itakama, and has
taken land of Amki. And sent men to
occupy Amki; kings of Khatta and of
Narima (Naharain) are destroying . . .

    (W. 119; S.B.A. xiii. 220; R.P. xvii. 90.)

We find here the echo of the earlier
affairs about Itakama, given in letters 107–
109. Probably recapitulated here by Rabimur because he had not corresponded with
the king before. But the same present news
is given by Ribaddi.

(189) RIBADDI to the king. Gubla in danger.
    Children and wood all sold to Yarimuta for
    food. Khabiri killed Aduna king of Ir-
    qata . . . seized Ardata, and take away
    the lands of Qutu, and kings of Mitani and
    Nakhrima . . .   (W. 79.)

The whole of northern Phoenicia, just to
the north of Tripoli, seems to have been
lost by this time.

(190) RIBADDI to the king. Desires troops,
    and that land may be put under city
    governors, and then they will have peace,
    and no longer write about R. and Yank-
    hamu.   (W. 98; B.O.D. 25.)

H

Next come more excuses from Aziru.

(191) AZIRI to the king. A. is slandered. King
wrote about Khani the envoy. A. explains
that he was staying at Tunip, and knew not
of K.'s coming. When he heard he started,
but did not overtake K. A.'s brother and
Bati-ilu waited upon K., and gave him full
supplies and animals. When A. came to
see the king, K. received him kindly. And
now king accuses A. of neglecting K. A.
appeals to the kings, gods, and the sun that
he really was at Tunip. King ordered A.
to rebuild Tsumur; but A. says kings of
Nukhashi are hostile, and are taking A.'s
cities by order of Khatib, so A. has not
rebuilt Tsumur, but will do so quickly.
Khatib took away half the implements and
all the gold and silver sent .by the king.
King asks why A. refused his envoy and
welcomed that of the Khatti; but A. will
give everything to an envoy.

(W. 51 ; S.B.A. xv. 372.)

Another letter of excuse is from Abdashirta, the father.

(192) ABDASHRATU to the king. A. guards
the whole land of Amurri for the king. A.
tells Pakhanati, his inspector, to bring a
guard to defend the king's land . . .
Amurru. . . . Ask Pakhanati if A. does
not defend Tsumuri and Ullaza. A. is
under P.   (W. 38 ; S.B.A. xv. 502.)

These letters show that the Amorite party of Abdashirta and his son Aziri were posing still as faithful subjects. This letter 192 gives the last mention of Ullaza. The excuse of Aziri for not receiving the king's envoy might hold good; but we know too well Aziri's reason for being at Tunip, from the previous wail of the people of Tunip about their fear of Aziri, in letter 170. Evidently Aziri felt quite strong enough to do as he chose, and to tell the king that he would rebuild Tsumura soon, without really troubling about it.

While Ribaddi was absent in Beyrut the people of Gubla wrote a municipal letter to the king. This is the third such letter from a community without any titular head, the others being from Irqata (159) and Tunip (170).

(193) People of GUBLA to the king. Tsumuri is captured and people of Gubla are slain. Ask for 240 men, 30 chariots, and 600 people of Kashi to defend Gubla. Biwari, the "gate-keeper" of the king, is killed. Pakhamnata will not listen. There is no food or grain for the troops . . . names Yankhama.   (W. 97 ; B.O.D. 24.)

This letter, though clearly addressed from the people of Gubla, yet lapses into personal expressions, "they will kill me," "I am anxious," and "Pakhamnata did not listen to me," showing probably the habit of the scribe in writing for Ribaddi and other officers. But the sequence of the letters points to Ribaddi being in Beyrut when this was written, and so agrees to its being a municipal letter as it is headed.

(194) [RIBADDI to the king.] Names Gubla; desires if no troops come that ships be sent to bring him alive to the king. Names Biwari. (W. 105.)

It is not likely that this Biwari is the same as Bikhura or Pakhura of Kumidi, as that person must rather be connected with the Paura who afterwards fought in the southern campaign about Jerusalem, and who cannot be the Biwari who was slain here.

Next we find letters of Ribaddi to various officials in Syria.

(195) RIBADDI to AMANAPPA. Asks why A. does not come with troops and take the land of Amurri. Amurri have a fort and no longer belong to Abdashirta; they hope day and night for troops that they may fall

on Aziri. All the governors hate Abda-shirta since he ordered people of Ammiya to slay their master and join the Khabiri. R. asks A. to tell all this to the king. A. knew R. and his fidelity in Tsumura.

(W. 57 ; S.B.A. xv. 355.)

(196) RIBADDI to KHAIAPA. Why delay in telling the king to occupy Tsumura? Abda-shirta is a dog, and the king's land goes to him to save its life, being endangered by the Khabiri. Send 50 yoke of horses and 200 men, and hold him in check at Shigata till troops come ; thus prevent him bringing Khabiri to take Shigata and Ambi.

(W. 54 ; R.P. xviii. 56.)

From these letters we see that the people of Amurri were not satisfied with Abda-shirta's advance, that there was a party against him, and that Ribaddi hoped to use that party for his overthrow. Aziri's con-quests and promotion of treachery had put all the other chiefs in fear, and a good body of opponents might be raised to attack him. This gleam of Egyptian hopes would be about the 12th year of Akhenaten ; and it may be some success at that time which is signalized by the captives of Kharu in the tomb of Huya, No. 1 at Tell el Amarna, dated in the 12th year.

29. *Ribaddi in Gubla.*

Next we find that Ribaddi went back from Beyrut to Gubla in order to face Aziri in his attack on Shigata and Gubla.

(197) RIBADDI to [KHAIAPA?]   Now that K. has entered Bît-tiri all is over.   When K. wrote to R. to go and occupy Tsumur, K. should know that the enemy are too strong for R.   Ambi is hostile; and the deputy and city governors are in alliance with Abdashirta's sons.   R. cannot march.
(W. 82; B.O.D. 23.)

This Beit Tiri to which Khaiapa retreated seems to be probably the ruin of *Et Tireh* on the foot of the hills behind Akka.   It seems as if, despairing of holding out against Aziri, the Egyptian officer had retreated southward, and taken up a position outside Akka on the hills, where he could command the approaches to that city.

(198) ARA . . . of Kumidi to the king.   Let the king enquire of Khamashni about A., who sent his son to Egypt to bring oil from the king.
(W. 141.)

This refers to some native ruler of Kumidi apparently, where also was an Egyptian officer, Bikhura, as we see in the next.

(199) RIBADDI to the king. Abdashirta long
afflicted R., who wrote to king's father for
troops to rescue the land. Aziru has
assembled Khabiri against Gubla. . . .
Appeals to Yankhama as witness. Names
Paya— . . . "they did not listen to the
words of Khaib, their father." Khaib has
delivered over Tsumura ; and let not the
king overlook the killing of the deputy. If
help does not come Bikhura will be unable
to hold Kumidi. . . . (W. 94 ; B.O.D. 18.)

This letter shows that Ribaddi, as well as
Akizzi (letter 111) had written to Amenhotep
III. about Aziru's hostility. In the next two
letters we see that Bikhura, not being able
to hold Kumidi, had yielded it up and joined
the enemy. He had been originally the
Egyptian deputy or officer, who was appealed
to by Itakama for help (letter 114).

(200) RIBADDI to the king. An unexampled
deed has been done against Gubla. Bikhura has sent Shuti men, who have slain
the Shirdanu. When the king writes
"Protect yourself," with whom is R. to
protect himself? Send back the three
people whom Bikhura, sent to Egypt,
namely Abdirama, Natan - Addu, and
Abdmilki. (W. 77 ; B.O.D. 20.)

(201) RIBADDI to the king. If king commands R. to defend the city, send provision and troops, for there are none. Pakhura has committed a great sin against R. by sending Shuti men and slaying the Shirdani, and sending three men to Egypt. Since then the city has rebelled against R.

(W. 100; R.P. xviii. 66.)

These letters show the use of auxiliaries by the Egyptians, the garrison of Gubla being of Shirdani, who, we know, are shown so frequently on the Egyptian monuments of the Ramesside times, and who were doubtless a Mediterranean people. Their greater vigour above the Egyptians is shown in the large camp scene on the pylon of the Ramesseum, where two of them are actively practising combat in the camp. The Shuti, whom the Egyptian deputy sent to attack them, were Sati or Bedawin, who were the Syrian auxiliaries when not enemies of the Egyptians. As we afterwards find this deputy acting faithfully in the southern campaign (letters 241, 254, 255) it seems that either he misunderstood Ribaddi or else the Shuti were acting irresponsibly and without his authority.

Next Gubla appears to be in serious straits, the presence of Ribaddi being quite insufficient to hold back the activity of Aziru.

(202) RIBADDI to the king. Abdashirta's enmity is bitter. Only Gubla and Biruna are left to R. All the Khabiri have become like the city of Ammi[a] . . . names Shuti and Shirdana. R. remains shut up and cannot get out of his city; the people are like a bird caught in a net, their sons and daughters and timber of houses are gone, sold to Yarimuta for food. If troops do not come in two months Abdashirta will capture the two cities.

(W. 64; R.P. xviii. 89.)

(203) RIBADDI to the king. R. protests his family fidelity, but the Khabiri oppress him. Sons, daughters, and [timber] are sold to Yarimuta for food. All R.'s cities, on hills and on sea, are lost to Khabiri, Gubla and two cities remain. Abdashirta has taken Shigata, and told men of Ammia to slay their lord, and they did so and became like Khabiri. And A. wrote to men of Bît Ninib to join in falling on Gubla. R. is like a bird caught in a net in Gubla. Amanappa is with the king, let him be asked.   (W. 55; S.B.A. xv. 351.)

These two letters were evidently written closely together, and just after the letters 200, 201, which were written in the first excitement of the slaughter of the Shirdana. The difficulties of famine, owing to the close siege, were being felt, and the neighbouring port of Yarimuta or Ramitha (Laodicea) being yet open, all valuable things—even the houses and the children— were being sold there for food. Ribaddi was feeling how hopeless it was to make head against Abdashirta, or even to get outside the gate of the city. So his favourite simile, of being like a bird caught in a net, is often used. The Bêt Ninib named here must have been near Gubla, and so cannot be the same as the Bêt Ninib which was near Jerusalem (letter 256).

The next letter seems to show increased destitution.

(204) RIBADDI to the king. R. has written similarly to the king, but was not attended to. Three years have passed, for two years grain was grown, now there is none. Sons, daughters, and [timber] of houses are no more, sold to Yarimuta for food. Let king

send grain in ships, and 400 men and 30
yoke of horses to Zu . . . to guard city.
Perhaps Yankhamu will be against giving
corn. Yapa-Addu has taken money, *x* is
with king, ask him about it. Corn formerly
given to Tsumura let them give to Gubla.
Asks for troops. Land is at disposal of
Yankhamu, . . . he has taken money for
children . . . to Yarimuta. King of Tana
(? or Tashu) has marched against Tsumura,
and was coming against Gubla, but turned
back for lack of water. If any prince
would join, R. would drive Abdashirta out
of Amurri. Since the king's father (Amenhotep III.) left Tsiduna lands have fallen to
the Khabiri. Names Mutshi(?) Milkuru(?)
handmaid of Ba'alat of Gubla.

(W. 69; R.P. xviii. 67.)

The king of Tana probably came from
the south of Tsumura, as he was going on
thence north to Gubla. Possibly we may
see in this name the district of Denniyeh
inland from Tripolis. It seems that Ribaddi
still kept up the hope of defeating Abdashirta if only he could get some assistance.
Here is again a reference to the troubles
beginning at the retirement of Amenhotep
III. The next two letters also refer to the
famine.

(205) RIBADDI to the king. R. is ordered to defend his city, but with whom shall he defend it? Formerly a garrison was there, and corn was sent from Yarimuta. But now Aziru has raided everything. Other princes hold their towns, but R.'s towns all belong to Aziru. "What dogs the sons of Abdashirta are! And they act according to their heart's wish and cause the king's cities to go up in smoke."

(W. 76; B.O.D. 19.)

(206) RIBADDI to AMANAPPA. Names Amurri and Mitani: desires A. to speak to Yankhamu. For three years no grain, and all is sold to Yarimuta.

(W. 66 and 90; B.O.D. 21.)

The difficulties yet increased, and the famine is even not noticed in the midst of more urgent perils.

(207) RIBADDI to the king. Since Amanappa came all the Khabiri have been set against R. by Abdashirta. R. asks for troops. Abdashirta has the city of Mar . . . and the foe is striving to take Gubla and Biruna, and all will fall to the Khabiri. Two cities left to R. they strive for, and R. is shut up in Gubla as a bird in a net.

(W. 60.)

This letter shows, like some earlier ones, that the wilder enemies of the Egyptians, such as the Khabiri, Suti, &c., had been their allies in the times of peace.

Domestic treachery now began to work, and Rabimur, who was formerly faithful (letters 187, 188), now began to give up hope of Egyptian help and to turn to Aziru.

(208) RIBADDI to the king. R. sent messenger to the court, but he returned empty without any troops. R. went to Khamuniri (Amunira), and his brother occupied Gubla in order to deliver it to Abdashirta's sons. And if no garrison is sent his brother will be hostile, and drive R. out of the city. R. cannot come to Egypt. Old age and disease press upon him. R. sent his son to the king and begs for troops for Gubla, which he still guards for the king, though his brother is inciting it to turn to the sons of Abdashirta. Let the king not neglect his city, for there is much silver and gold in it, and property in the temples. Let R. be allowed to live in Buruzilim. R. will go to Khamuniri if Gubla is lost; and he fears A.'s sons will attack Buruzilim if he goes to Khamuniri. R. now sends his son. (W. 71; R.P. xviii. 70.)

This Khamuniri or Amunira was, as we see in letters 216–218, the Egyptian governor of Beyrut, to whom Ribaddi was soon obliged to flee for refuge.

(209) RIBADDI to AMANAPPA.   Asks for 300 men to defend Gubla and to occupy Biruna, so that people may abandon Abdashirta.   (W. 68.)

(210) RIBADDI to the king.   Aziru has taken all but Gubla.   (W. 103.)

This taking of all the cities evidently does not include Beyrut, because that did not belong to Ribaddi, but was under its Egyptian governor, Amunira; but all of Ribaddi's cities were lost except Gubla. At last he fled to Beyrut for shelter, though he finally managed to get back to Gubla, and there he disappeared from sight.

30. *Ribaddi in Beyrut.*

We read from Beyrut :—

(211) RIBADDI to the king.   Abdashirta has taken all but two cities.   In Gubla he was like a bird caught in a net, and he is now in Biruna.   (W. 62.)

(212) RIBADDI to the king.   Only Biruna is left.   Names the Khatti.   Namiawaza fears the king.   Names prince of Kumidi.
                    (W. 63.)

Hence we see that in Beyrut he had some news through from the inland district. The letter is too much mutilated to follow the sense; but it seems as if the faithful Namiawaza was still at large, and Beyrut was not closely pressed. Another letter much mutilated belongs perhaps to some earlier period.

(213) *x* to the king. Tashu . . . is hostile . . . servants of my lord of Rukhizi. A messenger of the king has said, "In Mitani . . . and three or four kings treat as hostile (?) . . . king of Khatti." . . .
(W. 136.)

Rukhizi was the city of Arzawaya or Arzauia (letter 112), and is named with Dasha, who is probably the same as Tashu of this letter. Rukhizi is otherwise called Mikhiza in letter 75. This letter may perhaps best come in with the other late mention of that district in letter 212.

(214) *x* [RIBADDI ?] to the king. *y* [Rabimur (?), see 208] has taken Gubla. Let Yankhamu be asked. Abdashirta has come against *x*. Asks for 100 men and people from Kash and 30 chariots to defend the city until the king occupies Amurri.   (W. 137.)

(215) *x* to [AMANAPPA ?]. [RIBADDU (?) complaining of Rabimur (?)] Names Tsumuri. *y* has made treaty with prince of Kubli . . . "to all the Zukhluti people of your lord." . . . (W. 121.)

These fragments seem to belong to about this period, as Gubla had been lost to the opposite party when they were written. Of the Zukhluti we know no more; they may have been a class of auxiliaries.

We get more detail of Ribaddi's flight to Beyrut in the next three letters, which supplement the brevity of letters 211, 212.

(216) RIBADDI to the king. The men of Gubla and R.'s house and wife say, "Attach yourself to Abdashirta's son so that we may all have peace." But R. did not consent, but often asked for more troops. No message was returned, so R. went to treat with Ammunira, and establish friendship; but when he returned they had closed his house against him. R. is still steadfast, but if the king will not help he is a dead man. Two boys and two women of his have been given to the rebel.

(W. 96; S.B.A. xv. 362.)

Two earlier letters may be quoted here to show the position of Amunira. It should be noticed that he writes correctly Birutu, whereas Ribaddi generally writes Biruna.

(217) AMUNIRA of Birutu to the king. A. was ordered to place himself with the troops, and he did so with all his resources.
> (W. 128 ; S.B.A. xv. 366 ; B.O.D. 26.)

(218) AMUNIRA of Birutu to the king . . . of the king are all gone. . . .   (W. 129a.)

(219) *x* to the king. When the king's ships come to Birutu *x* will forward them . . . Biruna. . . .
> (W. 130.)

Amunira's version of Ribaddi's affairs is instructive, and clears up the condition of matters.

(220) [AMUNI]RA to the king. A. has heard the words of the tablet. A. keeps close guard and watches Birutu for the king. " As to the man from Gubla (Ribaddi) who is with me I am indeed guarding him until the king shall care for his servant." His (R.'s) brother, who is in Gubla, has given the sons of Ribaddi who is with me to the enemy of Amurri.
> (W. 129 ; S.B.A. xv. 368.)

This repeats about the treachery of Rabimur which Ribaddi states in letter 216, and which is alluded to in 214, 215.   It

I

seems, however, that Beyrut was even in more danger than Gubla, for the next news that we have is of Beyrut being taken, and the return flight of Ribaddi to Gubla, which he seems to have been able to re-enter safely, though he could hold it for but little longer.

31. *Ribaddi in Gubla.*

(221) RIBADDI to the king. Names Amma (= Ammia). Abdashirta is a dog, and attacked R., and has now taken Biruna, and will come against R. Shuarbi is the gate of Gubla. If the king will march A. will leave the gate, but R. cannot now get out of the door. If the king does not send troops Gubla will fall into A.'s hands, and all the king's lands as far as Mitsri (Egypt) will fall into the hands of the Khabiri. Behold, Gubla is not like other towns, Gubla is the faithful city.

(W. 65; B.O.D. 17.)

These statements of Beyrut being lost, of the close siege of Gubla, of its fall entailing the loss of all the coast down to Egypt, and of Gubla being the faithful city, all show that this is one of the last letters from North Syria.

(222) *x* [RIBADDI] to the king. Hostility strong, no provisions, and people will desert to Abdashirta's sons, and Ziduna and Biruta are hostile. Let the king occupy them that *x* may not have to yield his city. When the people withdraw the Khabiri will occupy it . . . Yankhami . . . (W. 92.)

(223) [RIBADDI] to the king. Names Tsumura. *y* has taken Gubla . . . "(for) 1000 of silver and 100 of gold he will depart from me, and he has taken all my cities, Gubla alone is left to me, and they are seeking to capture it, for I hear that he has united all the Khabiri ". . . . (W. 102.)

(224) RIBADDI to the king. Gubla alone is left , , , Behold Biruna . . . Behold my cities are lost . . . Mitani . . . Khabiri . . . Abdashirta. (W. 93.)

(225) RIBADDI to AMANABBI. Why has A. told R. to send messenger to receive men and chariots from Egypt? R. did so, but messenger returned alone. And Biruna has fallen to *y* and the Khabiri, although troops were there. And the enemy do not depart from the gate of Gubla . . .
(W. 67.)

These four letters end the history of northern Syria. Ribaddi flying from one city to another to animate the Egyptian resistance was at last reduced to Gubla alone, and then he disappears altogether. Whether he succeeded in fleeing down to Egypt, or capitulated to his foe Aziru, or was killed by treachery or capture, we have no light. His resistance was faithful and hardy; and the Egyptian yoke cannot have been very oppressive to Syria when a native would be thus faithful in the face of the greatest discouragement and opposition. The Egyptian power had finally departed from northern Syria after several generations of dominion, and there is only left the south Syrian war, where we shall see several of the former actors again continuing their support of the waning power of Egypt.

CHAPTER IV.

THE SOUTH SYRIAN WAR

32. *Abdkhiba in Trouble.*

ONE of the earliest letters of the troubles in Palestine is that from Baiya, who was son of Gulati, and whom we afterwards find seizing Gezer and Rabbath (letter 260), and taking prisoners (letter 261). In the peaceful times he had sent reports of fidelity to the king (letter 100).

(226) BAIYA to the king. If Yankhamu does not come this year the Khabiri will seize the country. (W. 230; B.O.D. 60.)

But the main series of letters from Palestine is that from Abdkhiba king of Jerusalem. These show that Jerusalem was not merely a Jebusite village made into a capital by David and Solomon, but was the capital of south Palestine from early times. From the accounts of the state of Palestine at the Israelite invasion it appears that the Amorites held most of the country, but this was apparently not the case in the XVIIIth Dynasty. On the contrary, they are never mentioned in the south at all. But the Israelites found Amorites in possession of Jerusalem, Hebron, Yarmuth, Lachish, and Eglon (Josh. x. 5). This southern extension of the Amorite power is probably the direct consequence of the rise of Aziru, the chief of the Amorites, who carried their rule from the land of Amurri, or the Lower Orontes, down to Gish in Galilee early in the present war (letter 116); and then seems to have spread on southward, until by the time of the Israelite invasion the Amorites were paramount in the whole of Palestine. This also accords with the prominence of the Amar in the triumphs of Ramessu III. on the walls of Medinet Habu, though he does not seem to have at all touched northern Syria. Apparently the earliest letter of Abdkhiba refers to trouble already arising.

(227) ABDKHIBA to the king. A. has been slandered, and accused of revolt. He was not an hereditary chief, but was set up by the king. He is slandered because he reproached the king's officer with favouring

the Khabiri. Yankhamu has taken away a garrison. Cities of the king under Ili-milki have fallen away. A. continually tells the officers that all the dependent princes will be lost. Let troops be sent, for the king has no longer any territory, the Khabiri have wasted all. "To the scribe of my lord the king—Abdkhiba your servant. Bring aloud before my lord the king the words, 'The whole territory of my lord, the king, is going to ruin.'"

(W. 179; R.P. xvii. 66.)

This last injunction to the scribe, to impress the facts on the king, is curious; it bears such a stamp of sincerity that it seems alive in its earnestness even now.

33. *Milkili and allies doubtful.*

This Ili-milki or Milk-ili wrote also to Egypt to clear his character.

(228) MILKILI to the king. Hostility against M. is powerful, and against Shuwardata. Let the king rescue the land from the Khabiri, or send chariots to remove the loyal. Names Yankhama.

(W. 170; R.P. xvii. 80.)

(229) MILKILI to the king. Yankhamu has taken 3(?)000 talents from M., and demanded his wife and sons that Y. might

kill them. M. asks for chariots to bring
him and family to the court.

(W. 171 ; B.O.D. 62.)

Here we see much what appeared in the
north, several parties, Abdkhiba, Yankhamu,
and Milkili, all acting in professed subjection
to Egypt, but all quarrelling for their own
success. The amount of 3000 talents seized
by Yankhamu seems prodigious, and is most
likely an error or exaggeration.

Shuwardata, mentioned above as an ally
of Milkili, also wrote to Egypt complaining
of troubles.

(230) SHUWARDATA to the king. S. was
invited to court, but cannot come. Yankhamu knows his troubles. Let the king
rescue him. Thirty towns are hostile, and
his enemies are powerful.   (W. 166.)

Of another ally of Milkili, his son-in-law
Tagi, an early letter belongs to the beginning
of the troubles, when a brother was wounded.
Letters, during the peace, were received from
Tagi (80, 81).

(231) TAGI to the king. T.'s brother has been
wounded, so T. does not wait to send his
letter with his brother's. T. is now trying
to send caravans to Egypt.

(W. 189; B.O.D. 70.)

34. *Abdkhiba attacked.*

But Tagi was soon in opposition along
with Milkili. The following letter is probably
from Abdkhiba, though Winckler attributes
to Addumikhir.

(232) [ABDKHIBA?] to the king.   What has
A. done to Milkili that he should attack
him?   M. gave servants to his father-in-
law, Tagi.   Names Milkili and the sons of
Lapaya.   (W. 186.)

The next is certainly from Abdkhiba, as it
was written from Jerusalem.

(233) [ABDKHIBA to the king.] . . . Urusalim.
If this land is the king's, why is not Khazati?
Ginti-kirmil is fallen to Tagi, and men of
Ginti are fallen.   And we will conquer in
order that they may not give Lapaya and
his lands to the Khabiri.   Milkili sent to
Tagi and sons. . . . . people of Qilti.   We
will deliver Urusalim.   The garrison sent
by Khaya was taken by Adda-mikhir to
Khazati.   (W. 185 ; R.P. xvii. 73.)

Here we see that the hill country west of
Jerusalem was lost, also the coast town Gaza.
The next letter gives more detail.

(234) ABDKHIBA to the king. A. has been
slandered, but protests his fidelity. When
Shuta, the officer, came, A. sent 21 women
and 20 men as a present to the king. Land
of Shiri, as far as Ginti-kirmil, its princes
are wholly lost, and fight against A. So
long as ships were on the sea the king
occupied land of Nakhrima and land of
Kash. Now the Khabiri occupy the cities.
Not one prince remains, all are ruined.
Turbatsu was slain at the gate of Zilu.
Servants conspire against Zimrida, of
Lakisi. Yapti-Addi was slain at the gate
of Zilu. Asks for troops to Urusalim, or
all will be lost. If not, desires to be fetched
away with his brothers, to the king. "To
the scribe of my lord the king,—Abdkhiba,
your servant. At your feet I fall. Bring
these words plainly before my lord, the
king; 'I am your faithful servant.'"

(W. 181 ; R.P. xvii. 68.)

This letter shows that not only the west,
but the north of Jerusalem was lost. The
land of Shiri, as far as Ginti-kirmil, is
Shaaraim (Heb.), *Khurbet es Sairah*, which
is four miles nearer Jerusalem than En
Gannim (Heb.), *Khurbet Umm Jina*, and
these "gardens" would naturally be vine-
yards—kirmil—as . it is in the Vale of
Sorek, "the choice vine." Then Zilu,

where two chiefs, Turbatsu and Yapti-Addi, were slain, is Zelah (Heb.) north of Jerusalem.

(235) ABI . . . . to the general.   Shipti-Addi and Zimrida demand the city; and Shipti-Addi spoke to Zimrida about Abishiarami.   (W. 219.)

This is the celebrated tablet found at Tell Hesy; and from its locality it doubtless refers to Zimrida, of Lachish, and not to Zimrida of Sidon. The other mention of Shipti-Addi is in letter 56, with Yankhamu; but the latter appears in both northern and southern letters, so that proves nothing as to place.

35. *Fighting round Gezer.*

We next turn to the prince of Gezer, west of Jerusalem, close to Ginti.

(236) YAPAKHI to the king. Y. is obedient, but has suffered from the Suti people.
                                          (W. 206; B.O.D. 51.)

(237) YAPAKHI of Gazri to the king. Y.'s youngest brother rebels, and occupied Mu . . khazi, allied with the Khabiri, who are now hostile to Y. Asks for instructions.
                                          (W. 205; B.O.D. 50.)

(238) YAPAKHI of Gazri to the king. Asks for help, as the Khabiri are powerful, and let the king rescue him from the Khabiri.

(W. 204; B.O.D. 49.)

We have seen before some mention of Lapaya, who in letter 232 seems to have been faithful. He fell into trouble, however, as follows :—

(239) LAPAYA to the king. The city was taken by an attack of the enemy, although in peace, and with an officer of the king with L. (W. 162; B.O.D. 61.)

The next, however, shows that he found it expedient to join the enemy, and that his next affair was attacking Yapakhi of Gezer.

(240) LAPAYA to the king. L. is a faithful servant, and has been slandered. Is it an offence that he has entered Gazri, and levied the people? Let the king take all that L. and Milkili have, and then decide between him and M. King wrote asking if Dummuia had joined the Khabiri. L. had handed him to Adda-Dan. If king demanded L.'s wife he would send her; or if he ordered L. to run a sword of bronze into his heart he would do it.

(W. 163; R.P. xvii. 78.)

Here we see that Lapaya was against Gezer, and also against Milkili. This seems to be another three-cornered fight, in which no one quite knew who sided with Egypt. Another letter has lost the name, but belongs to this time.

(241) x to king. Y. has taken silver, people, sheep, and everything from the cities the king gave to x, who writes through Pakhura. Names Tagi and Lapaya.   (W. 191.)

Pakhura was at first in North Galilee, but he appears later on at Gaza. This shift southward, like the shift of the activities of Yankhamu from north to south, is important as showing that the southern war was not simultaneous with the northern, and probably, therefore, succeeded it.

36. *Fighting round Megiddo.*

After Lapaya rebelled in the south, at Gezer, he seems to have gone up through Samaria to Megiddo. First we have a letter from the chief of Megiddo early in the affair.

(242) BIRIDIYA of Makidda to the king. Sent 30 cattle, but is attacked by some one.
    (W. 194.)

(243) BIRIDIYA to the king. Two sons of Lapaya gave money to the Khabiri.
    (W. 192.)

(244) BIRIDIYA to the king. Since the troops left, Lapaya has attacked B., who cannot go out of Magidda. Let the king rescue his city, that Lapaya may not take it.

(W. 195; R.P. xvii. 81.)

(245) BIRIDIYA to the king. B. is defending Makida, but powerful is the enmity of the Khabiri. (W. 193; R.P. xvii. 82.)

The following may probably be also from Biridiya, but it is only a second tablet of a letter, and the beginning cannot now be identified.

(246) *x* to the king. *x* agreed with his brothers to capture Lapaya and bring him to the king, and go with Yashdata to Egypt, for Y. is loyal, and goes into battle with *x*. But Zurata took Lapaya out of Magidda and said to *x* that Z. would send him by ship to the king. But Zurata sent him home from Khinatuna and took the money for his ransom. Zurata also let Addumikhir go.

(W. 196; B.O.D. 72.)

(247) YARTA or YASHDATA to the king. People of Takh. . . . have raided the cattle of Y. who is with Biridiya.

(W. 197; B.O.D. 59.)

This shows that Zurata or Surata of Akka (letter 119) was interfering, professedly in Egyptian interests, but really for his own profit: Akka being a port, he naturally proposed to send Lapaya by sea. His taking him over the Jordan to Kanawat to release him, is in accord with Shutatna son of Sharatu of Akkaiu seizing the caravan from Burnaburyash in Kanawat (letter 124). The princes of Akka seem to have ruled the country across to Bashan. The writer of 246 may be read as Yashda . . . and is probably the Yashdata of the previous letter. The people of Takh . . . may be of Takhida, where Ribaddi's messenger was stopped on the way from Beyrut to Egypt. If so it must be looked for near Megiddo.

37. *Shuwardata in Trouble.*

We now turn to Shuwardata, who we have seen was an Egyptian ally (letter 230), and was being attacked by the Khabiri (letter 228).

(248) SHUWARDATA to the king. S. asks for troops to rescue him.   (W. 199.)

(249) SHUWARDATA to the king. S. in trouble, wants troops.   (W. 201.)

(250) SHUWARDATA to the king. The country rebels and Qilti is lost.
                                                      (W. 167.)

(251) SHUWARDATA to the king. King ordered S. to war against Qilti. He has done so, and is successful. Why did Abdkiba write to Qiltites saying, "Take money and join me"? Let the king know that Abdkhiba has taken the city of S. Lapaya is dead who took cities of S. Lapaya was allied with Abdkhiba, and robbed cities of S.
(W. 165; S.B.A. xi. 348; R.P. xvii. 77.)

This last letter must then be after letters 240–246, describing Lapaya's warfare.

Of a chief in northern Palestine we obtain a little light.

(252) . . . .WARZANA prince of Khazi to the king. Prince of Tushulti has attacked him. Khabiri are taking cities, including Makhzi . . . ti, and burnt it. Khabiri betake themselves to Amankhatbi. Khabiri have occupied Sigi . . . and burnt it. The house of Bil-garib (?) is rescued; . . . . rescued from the city of Mati . . . Ushtiru is taken by the Khabiri and burnt; and they will occupy Khazi. Amankhatbi is an enemy. (W. 134; R.P. xvii. 85.)

(253) x to king, from city of Tu . . . Khabiri are enemies. Names Amankhatbi, and city of Khabi. . . . (W. 135.)

The district of this letter is not clear. Tushulti seems like the Tasuret or Tasulet of Tahutmes III., which is almost certainly *Teiasir* near Shechem in Samaria. But on the other hand, Khazi is probably the same here as in 107, where the geography apparently fixes it to *el'Azziyeh* between the Jordan and the Litâny. And Makhzi . . . ti looks like Mikhiza, the city of Arzawaya on the south of Hermon. If so, Ushtiru would be *Shtora*, between Beyrut and Damascus. The second letter seems to belong to the first, Tu . . . being Tushulti, and possibly Khabi a mistake for Khazi.

38. *Abdkhiba Failing.*

We now turn back to Abdkhiba, in a later letter, written after the letters 233, 234 from him ; after 239, 240 from Lapaya ; after 244 from Biridiya ; after 246 on Lapaya's capture ; and after 251 on Lapaya's death. In this Lapaya seems to be dead, and his sons acting alone.

(254) ABDKHIBA to the king. All the countries are hostile, Gazri, Asqaluna, and Lakisi ; if no troops are sent, nothing will be left to the king. Milkili and the sons of Lapaya

are delivering land to the Khabiri. A. is innocent about the Kashi (who seem to have been plundering). Until the officer Pauru went to Urusalim Adaya was in revolt. Caravans of the king were robbed at Yaluna, so A. cannot forward them. "To the scribe of my lord the king,— Abdkhiba your servant. At your feet I fall. I am your servant. Bring plainly before my lord, the king, these words, 'I am an officer of the king.' May you be very well." And if A. has done evil to the Kashi, let A. be killed.

(W. 180; R.P. xvii. 74.)

This letter has the curious little postscript to the scribe, like most of his other letters; and it seems as if the cuneiform scribe at Tell el Amarna were a personal friend of Abdkhiba's, and was expected to specially interfere on his behalf with the king.

(255) ABDKHIBA to the king. Milkili has revolted to the sons of Lapaya, and the sons of Arzawa. Milkili and Tagi have taken Rubuta. Puuru is in Khazati. Let Yan-khamu be sent. "To the king's scribe, —Abdkhiba your servant. Bring the message plainly before the king. May it be very well indeed with you. I am your servant." (W. 182; R.P. xvii. 71.)

(256) ABDKHIBA to the king. Milkili and
Shuwardata have taken soldiers of Gazri,
Gimti, Qilti, and occupied the region of
Rubuti. Men of Qilti have taken Bît-
Ninib belonging to Urusalim. If no troops
are sent the land will belong to the Khabiri.
(W. 183 ; R.P. xvii. 72.)

These last three letters of Abdkhiba close
his correspondence. We see how he was
hemmed in more and more. Gezer, Ashkelon, and Lachish lost; the caravans
plundered at Ayalon ; then Gimzu, joining
the enemy in taking Rabbath ; and a town
by Jerusalem taken. Arzawa named here
is probably Arzawaya, formerly of Mikhizi
by Hermon. Puuru, who was the officer in
Gaza, is most likely Pakhura, or Bikhura,
who was the officer in northern Palestine
somewhat earlier. It seems likely that
Abdkhiba himself joined the Khabiri at
last, as most of these princes and chiefs
did when they saw that help could not be
had from Egypt.

39. *Loss of South Palestine.*

The following letter is from a man otherwise unknown.

(257) ADDU-ASHARIDU to the king. Two
sons of Lapaya rebel, and desired A. to

join against men of Gina, who killed their
father, or else they would fight him. Asks
that an officer be sent to Namyawaza to
order him to fight the sons of Lapaya.
They ask A. to fight the king, as Lapaya
did when he besieged Shuna . ., and
Bur . . . ., and Kharabu, and Gitirimu . . .
Messengers of Milkili also stir rebellion.

(W. 164 ; R.P. xvii. 83.)

The places named here seem to belong
to the Joppa region ; Shuna . . . may be
Shunama ; Kharabu, El Khurab ; and
Gitirimu . . . Gathrimmon. This shows
that Lapaya probably took Joppa. We
see here how Namyawaza has drifted down
into the southern seat of war, like so many
other of the northern fighters, Arzawaya,
Pakhura, Maia, Rianappa, &c. This shows
that the southern war succeeded the northern,
and was, probably, a sort of running fight
from the Orontes down to the Egyptian
frontier.

Addu-daian was another personage about
this time, but his locality is unknown.

(258) [ADDU]DAIAN to the king. Defends his
    city. (W. 275.)
(259) ADDU-DAIAN to the king. Names
    Yâb . . . . and Kaya . . . . ; asks for 30
    men, and will come to Egypt. (W. 240.)

(260) ADDU-DAIAN to the king. Ordered to defend his city and will do so. City of Tumurka rebels, and A. has fortified Mankhatishum; but Maya has taken it from him, and put officer in it. Asks for order to Rianap to return it to A. Biia, son of Gulati, has taken Gazri and Rubuti. Ransoms to *x* were 30 of silver, to Biia 100 of gold.   (W. 239; M.A.F. vi. 279.)

(261) *x* to the king. Biia son of Gulati took brothers of *x*, whom *x* had sent to serve in Yapu. If *x* is ordered to give his city to Biia he would do so, and go to serve the king.   (W. 178; B.O.D. 71.)

From these letters it seems that Addudaian was in the south of Judea. He names Gezer and Rabbah. Tumurka is probably Tumrah, near Gaza; and Mankhatishum seems from its length to be a compound name, including that of the Wady Menakh, near Gezer. Biia was formerly an Egyptian subject, as in letter 100, where he obeys Maya, and letter 226.

(262) *x* to the king. Magdalim and Kuatsbat are hostile; and Abbikha heads an insurrection.   (W. 281; B.O.D. 73.)

This city of Kuatsbat seems to be Cozeba of the Hebrew, now *Kueiziba*, near Halhul.

This Magdalim must be a fortress, or tower, in the Judean hills; but the name does not seem to have survived like the Magdala in the north.

(263) DAGANTAKALA to the king. Asks for rescue from the Khabiri and the Shuti.
(W. 216; B.O.D. 47.)

(264) DAGANTAKALA to the king. Father and grandfather were obedient, and D. will listen and obey. (W. 215; S.B.A. xiii. 327.)

This chief seems to have been in the south Palestine land, as the name of the god Dagon is used by him. Beth Dagon—now Dajun—is six miles S.E. of Joppa, and Dagon was worshipped at Gaza and Ashdod.

(265) NINUR to the king. Land has fallen away to the Khabiri, who have sent to Aialuna, and to Tsarkha . . . . two sons of Milkili
. . . .   (W. 173.)

(266) [NINUR] to the king. Asks to be rescued from the Khabiri. City of Tsapuna has been captured.   (W. 174.)

The latter letter is doubtless from Ninur, as in both she addresses the king as his hand-maid, and writes in the same style.

The district of this queen was evidently

in Judea, as she mames Milkili, and the attack on Ayalon and Zorah, in the hills, half-way from Jerusalem to the coast. The city of Tsapuna is therefore somewhere near there, and Siffîn, north of Ayalon, seems to correspond to this. It is certain that these letters must come late in the history, as the position of the Khabiri corresponds to that of the last of Abdkhiba's letters.

This last letter may belong to Galilee, but cannot be safely placed.

(267) *x* to king.   Brother of *x* has rebelled in Tubikhi, and gone to besiege cities . . . . . lands of Amurri . . . . . garrisons all gone . . . . . towns belong to Khabiri. Asks for help to retake Tubikhi.   (W. 127.)

40. In taking a general view of these letters, and the history that they show, we may notice some broad conclusions. The gradually shifting of the peoples down Syria southward is regular and clear. In the early part of these letters the Khita, Hittites, are in the far north, and only one or two princes have established themselves southward. The Hittite prince who went farthest south at that time was that on the mountains of Igaid (letter 1) in the Lebanon; having come

from the mountainous north it was natural that he should not do like other Syrians and settle in the fertile low plains, but rather on the colder mountain range. Then later the Khatti in general came south with Aziri, and plundered on the coast around Gubla (letter 152). After this age, about 1375 B.C., the Khatti advanced so that their chief city was Qedesh by Lake Homs, and Ramessu II. only obtained a frontier just beyond Beyrut by his fighting with them.

The Amurri, Amar, or Amorites show a similar and more complete shifting southward. Originally from the references here we glean that Amurri or Martu was the main part of the Orontes valley. Then in the time of Ramessu II. they appear side by side with the Khita at Qedesh. Later, the war of Ramessu III., which was mainly in southern Syria, found the Amar throughout that region. Lastly, when the Hebrews came in they found the "five kings of the Amorites" in Judea from Jerusalem down to Hebron and Eglon in the south. Here there is a continuous advance, and this is of value as bearing on the date of the Hebrew invasion. Had it been anywhere before Ramessu II. we ought not to find Amorites so far south, for there is not a single mention of the Amurri or of their chiefs Abdashirta and Aziru in the whole of the letters from Palestine, though they are the main factors in the north Syrian letters. We must, therefore, place all the accounts of the Hebrew conquest as after these letters and after the war of Ramessu II., at, in fact, the latest stage of the Amorite movement southward.

41. Another noticeable point is the variety of government in Syria at the time of this correspondence. Five different forms of government can be traced.

(1) *Chiefs appointed* by the king of Egypt, such as Ramman-nirari's grandfather (letter 36), and Yabitiri of Gaza and Joppa (letter 101).

(2) *Hereditary chiefs*, as Ramman-nirari (letter 36), Itakama (letter 114), Shumaddu (letter 126), and Aziri.

(3) *Female rule*, as by Ninur in Judea (letters 265, 266) reminding us of Deborah judging in Judea.

(4) *Elective chiefs*. Abdkhiba of Jerusalem repeatedly uses the formula, "Neither my father nor my mother appointed me in this place. The strong arm of the king

established me over my father's territory."
At first sight this would seem to be merely
a statement of his being the king's nominee.
But the writer of the Epistle to the Hebrews
had some document containing a similar
statement about another king of Jerusalem,
Melkizedek, being "without father, without
mother, without genealogy." (Heb. vii. 3.)
Such cannot be a coincidence when it concerns two kings of the same city, and is a
phrase never known elsewhere. We must
recognize in it a formula familiar at Jerusalem, and so quoted by Abdkhiba in referring
his elevation to the king. It is the formula
of an elective rule distinctly, and shows that
the main city of south Palestine for several
centuries was familiar with elected chiefs.

(5) *Municipal government.* This occurs
in three cities. Irqata addresses a letter
from "Irqata and its elders" (letter 159).
Dunip also addresses the king as "The
inhabitants of Dunip" (letter 170). And in
the absence of Ribaddi, Gubla managed its
own affairs and wrote from "The people
who are occupying (?) Gubla" (letter 193).
With these we may compare the deputation
from "the elders and all the inhabitants"

of Gibeon. (Josh. ix. 11.)   It is clear that
though government by chiefs was the more
usual, yet municipalities existed under the
Egyptian rule, much as they did in Asia
Minor and other countries under Roman
rule.

42. BIOGRAPHICAL OUTLINES OF PRINCIPAL PERSONS

ABDASHIRTA (B), ABDASHIRTA'S SONS (S), and AZIRI (Z), all linked together.

(The above are all variants of the name of one
commissioner.)

(The above all act as Egyptian commissioner, and seem to be probably all variants of one name.)

L

43. INDEX OF PERSONS

The star shows a change of allegiance from Egypt to Syria.

Irshappa, 1,*
Itakama, v. Biog. outline
Itilluna, 30,*

Kallimasin, 13, 14, (15?), 16, 17,*
Karaindash, 19,*
Kasi, 14,*
Kaya . . . ., 259,*
Khabi, * 184
Khai, Khaiapa, Khay, Khaib, v. Biog. outline
Khamashi, 11, 12, 21,*
Khamashni, 198,*
Khamuniri, v. Amunira
Khani. 7, 64, 147, 191,*
Kharamashi, 6,
Khatib, 148, 149, 150,* 155, 191
Khiziri, 99,*
Khuaa, 21,*
Kidinramman, 23,*
Kunia, 30,*
Kurigalzu, 20, 21,*
Kuzuna, 126,*

Lapaya, v. Biog. outline
Liya, * 147
Lupakku, * 110

Maia, 97, 99, 100, 160,* 260
Malia, * 147
Mani, 5, 6, 7, 9, 10, 11, 12, 144,*
Mazipalali, 11,*
Mikhuni, 21,*
Milkili, v. Biog. outline
Milkuru, 157, 204
Mutaddi, 118
Mutshi? (fem.), 157, 204
Mutzu 41

Namyawaza v. Biog. outline
Natanaddu, 200,
Nimmakhi, * 147
Ninur (fem.), 265, 266. *
Nizag, 11,*
Nurtuya . . . . ma, 176,*

Pakhamnata, 163,* 192, 193
Pakhura, v. Biog. outline
Paluia, * 150,
Paluma, * 147
Pamakhu, * 22
Pashtummi, 30,*
Pauru, v. Pakhura
Paya . . . ., 199
Perizzi, 10, 11, 12,*

Pirkhi, * 4
Puaddi, 72, 73, 74, *
Ramman-nirari, 36, *
Rabimur,   187,   188, *
    (215), (220)
Rianapa, 72, 96, 260, *
Ribaddi, v. Biog. out-
    line
Riqa, 13, *
Rusmania, 45, *

Shaba . . . ., 51, *
Shabi-ilu, 160, *
Shakhshikhashikha, 73
Sharatu, v. Zurata
Sharru, * 147
Shatiya, 68, *
Shindishugab, 19, *
Shiptiaddi, 56, 57, * 235
Shipturi, 42, *
Shubandi,   63   to   67,
    136, *
Shumadda, * 124, * 125,
    126
Shumukha . . . ., 52, *
Shuta, 16, 122, 234, *
Shutarna (king), 5, 11, *
Shutarna (governor), 37,
    38, *
Shutatna, v. Zatatna
Shuwardata, 86, 87, 228,

230,   248   to   251,   *
    256
Subayadi, 137, *
Surashar, 50, *
Surata, v. Zurata
[Su]warzana, 252, *

Tadua, 118, *
Tadukhipa, 8, 9, 10, 11, *
Tagi, 80, 81, 231, * 232,
    233, 241, 255
Takhmaini, 81, *
Takua, 36
Tarkhumdaraush, 1, *
Tashu . . . ., * 213
Tiuwati, * 112
Tsalma, 21, 22, *
Tunip-ipri, 4, *
Turbazu, 234, *
Turbikhaza, 165, *
Tuya, * 147

Ushbarra, 30, *

Yab . . . ., 52, 259, *
Yabaia, 160
Yabitiri, 101, *
Yabni-ilu, 97, *
Yadiaddu, 170, *
Yakhzibaia, 104, 105, *
Yama, 135, *

Yamilki, *v.* Abimilki, 185
Yamiuta, 106, *
Yankhamu, *v.* Biog. outline
Yapa-addi, *v.* Biog. outline
Yapakhi, 236, 237, 238
Yapakhi-addi, 171, 174,*
Yaptiaddu, 234, *
Yashdata, 246, 247, *
Yashuia, 118, *
Yiktasu, 54, *
Yishiari, * 147

Yitya, 90 to 96, *
Yuni, 9, *

Zaqara, 13, *
Zatatna, 120, 121, 122, * 124, *
Zida . . . ., 2, *
Zimrida, *v.* Biog. outline
Zirdayashda, * 122
Zishamini, 46, *
Zitana, 110, *
Zitriyara, 58, 59, 60, *
Zurata, 119, * 124, 246
Zu . . . ., 204, *

EGYPTIAN KINGS NAMED

Khuri = Napkhuriya, 3

Manakhbiia (Tahutmes III.), 36
Manakhbiria (Tahutmes IV.), 170
Mimmuria (Amenhotep III.), 9, 12

Napkhuria (Amenhotep IV.), 10, 11, 12, 18, 19, 20, 21, 22, 35, 124
Nimmuria (Amenhotep III.), 1, 4, 5, 6, 7, 8, 11, 13, 14, 16, 17, 111, 112, (204)

Tii (Tyi), 9, 10, 11

44. INDEX OF PLACES

Gagaya, 13, *
Gar, * 118
Gazri, 77, 237, 238, *
240, 254, 256, 260
Gimti, * 256
Gina, 257, *
Ginti-kirmil, * 233, 234
Giti-rimuna, * 257
Gizza, * 116
Gubbu, 61, *
Gubla, 147, 152, 156,
158, 161, 163, 164, 167,
168, 171, 186, 187, 188,
189, 193, 194, 199, 202,
203, 204, 207, 208, 209,
210, 211, 214, 215, 216,
220, 221, 223, 224, *
225

Igaid, 1, *
Ikhibni (omitted by W.;
B. 27)
Inishatsi(ri), 60, *
Irqata, 158, 159, 160, *
188, 189

Karduniyash, 13, 39,
41, *
Kashi, 156, 162, 172,
193, 214, 234, 254
Khabi . . . 253, *

Khabiri . . *in north*, 114,
115, * 116, 134, 136,
138, 140, 141, 142, 145,
155, 157, 163, 166, 172,
175, 183, 189, 195, 196,
199, 202, 203, 204, 207,
221, 222, 223, 224, 225,
226; *in south*, 227, 228,
233, 234, 237, 238, 240,
243, 245, 252, 253, 254,
256, 263, 265, 266, 267
Khalunni, * 116
Khanigalbat, 6, 11, 13,
35, 41,
Kharabu, * 257
Khashabu, 108,
Khasugari (omitted by
W.; B. 10)
Khatat, * 170
Khatti, 1, 2, 3, * 4, 33,
36, 107, 108, 109, 110,
111, 112, 148, 149, 150,
152, 156, 178, 188, 191,
212, 213
Khawini, * 118
Khazati, 233, 255, *
Khazi, 107, 137, 252, *
Khazura, 70, 71, * 183
Khikubta, 164, *
Khinatuna, * 124, * 246
Khinianabi, * 118
Kinakhaiu, 20,

156   INDEX OF PLACES

45. IDENTIFICATION OF PLACES

Italic names are modern Arabic forms.
Kh., often prefixed, is *Khurbet*, and shows an ancient
ruin to exist at the place.

ABITU occurs in a group of names which
must be considered together. The history
in the letter 116 is that Biridashya stirs up
Yanuh in the hinterland of Tyre, and then,
being afraid of Namyawaza coming down
from Kumidi by the Litâny, he boldly
struck across to the Hauran, brought up
forces of Bozrah, &c., and compelled N. to
retreat from Kumidi (on the Beyrut and
Damascus road) into Damascus, in order to
save that from the rebels. Then Aziru's
troops in Gish are brought up, either to the
bend of the Litâny, or on the Damascus
road, to Shaddu (not identified), to block
Namyawaza from reaching the Tyrian region.
Thus Gish was destroyed, and the territory
of Abitu will be taken. This points to
Abitu being S.W. of the line from Gish

159

to Yanuh, and this agrees to *Kh. Abdeh*, 15 S. of Tyre, 16 W. of Gish.

ADURI occurs in another group, 118. The cities of the land of Gar are Udumu, Aduri, Araru, Mishtu, Magdali, and Khini-anabi. There is no general indication of known locality, but most of these names are found west of the lake of Tiberias. The land of Gar is named in "the going up to Gur which is by Ibleam," and which led to Megiddo (2 Kings ix. 27); a phrase which belongs to a whole region, like "the entering in of Hamath." This "going up" must be the valley of Jezreel, and the land of Gar therefore about Nazareth. Here are found Udumu (Adamah *Heb.*, *Damieh*, 5 S.W. Tiberias), Aduri (*Et Tireh*, 14 W.S.W. Tiberias), Araru (*Ararah*, 8 S.W. Megiddo, the key to that city in the Tahutmes war), Mishtu (*Kh. Mushtah*, 14 W.N.W. Tiberias), Magdali (Magdala, *Mejdel*, 3 N.W. Tiberias), and Khinianabi (or 'Enanab, Winckler) may be Hananieh (*Kefr 'Anân*, 12 N.W. Tiberias). After this it is said Tsarqi, Khawani, and Yabishi were captured. Ya-bishi must be Yabesh Gilead (12 S.E. Bethshean), Khawani agrees to *Kh. Kâûn*, opposite across the Jordan (6 S. Bethshean), and Tsarqi is probably a *zerqa*, or dark place, a colour-name often found, though hardly the Jebel Zerqa 20 S.E. of Jabesh.

AKHLAMI are named with the king of Kardunyash, a people known to the Assyrians between Babylon and Nineveh (No. 39).

AKKA is undoubtedly *Akka*, Gr. Akko.

ALASHYA. This has been well proposed to be Cyprus, and looking to the abundance of copper it can hardly be doubted. One good indication should be sought; in No. 30 the Lycians plunder the city of Zikhru in Alasiya.

AMBI. This occurs grouped with other names. In clvi. there is the list of coast places, Ullaza, Ardata, Yikhliya, Ambi, and Shigata; and other letters name the ships of Ambi and Shigata. Ullaza is linked with Tsumura (155, 162, 165, 192), and the next port to Simyra is *Mina Kabusi*, and at the foot of the hill behind this is *El Usy*, or *Huzeh*, which is, therefore, probably very close to the site of Ullaza, and may well be it. Shigata at the other end of the list can hardly be other than Tell Sukat on the

M

Nahr Sukat 3 miles S. of Gibleh. The name of Ambi is not seen now, but by being linked with Shigata it is probably the next port, Baldeh, 4 miles S. There are but a small number of ports along this coast, and they leave, therefore, but little uncertainty when an associated point is already known. Yikhliya is probably *Qleiât*, 13 N.E. of Tripoli, and 5 N.E. of Ardata.

AMKI has been connected with the 'Amk plain by Antioch, but without any proof in favour of this more than the many other plains or valleys generically called 'Amk (*ghamyq*, deep, dark coloured), such as 'Ammîk (19 S.E. Beyrut), 'Amûqa (10 N. Capernaum), 'Amqa (8 N.E. Akka), Nahr Ghamkeh (by Ruad), &c. The references to Amki are mainly about an attempt by Biridashya (?) of Khashabu and Ildaya of Khazi to seize cities there, and their repulse by Itakama, prince of Kinza, and the Khatti (107–9, 188); Akizzi of Qatna refers to Itakama as hostile in the land of Ubi; Damascus is in Ubi, and appeals for help as Qatna does. And Nukhashi, Ni, Zinzar, and Kinanat are faithful (112). The region of Biridashya was in north Galilee, as noticed under Abitu, his activities lying west to Yinuama, and east to Ashtarti. Here there is not a single reference to any coast town; evidently the whole group is in the Orontes-Jordan valley. Damascus is the fixed point; Ubi (Egn. Aup?) must be the Damascus plain. In the region of Biridashya we must fix Khashabu as the Hôshaba valley of Banias, the capital being probably Banias. The other allied capital, Khazi, must be near; and a key of the country is Kh. 'Azziyeh (9 W.N.W. Banias), between the bend of the Litâny and the source of Jordan, one of the most important strategic points. The only great plain that these would command would be the Bukeiah up the Litâny, where *'Ammîk* stands (19 S.E. Beyrut). Itakama held Kinza himself, and Gidshi (a Qedesh) had belonged to his father (cviii.). For him to repel this north-ward movement he must have been to the north of 'Ammîk; his Qedesh then must be that of Lake Homs, and cannot be that by Lake Huleh. His Kinza is probably lost to sight in one of the many Kneseh (church) names in the Baalbek region. There are three places that might be Qatna, Tell Kateineh (by Lake Homs), Qatana

(14 W. Damascus), Kh. Kataneh (5 E.N.E. Safed). The first would be in Itakama's power, and too far from Damascus for Akizzi; the last would have no relation to Nukhashi, Ni, and Zinzar, with Itakama cutting communications at Qedesh. Hence the Qatana by Damascus must be the seat of Akizzi. Lapuna, which joined Itakama in attacking Qatna, is probably Halbûn (13 N.N.W. Damascus). This completes this group of associated names.

AMMIA. This country cut off Ubi (112), and was therefore somewhere west of it. Aziru seized Ammia, Ardata, and Ni, also Irqata and Tsumura (187-8, 195), and the men of Ammiya were stirred to slay their lord (203). The region thus indicated would be the upper part of the Orontes valley, and might thus be connected with the land of Hamath, or *Hamah*.

AMURRA is probably the middle and lower parts of the Orontes, on looking to all the connections; but it certainly covered a wide region.

ARARU, see ADURI.

ARDATA, known as Orthosia, *Arthûsi* (9 N.E. Tripoli).

ARSAPI, probably *Reseph*.

ARWADA known as Arvad, Aradus (Gr.), *Ruad*.

ASHTARTI joined with Bozrah and Golan; evidently Ashteroth (29 E. Tiberias).

ASQALUNA, known as Ashkelon.

ASSHUR, Assyria.

AYALUNA, known as Ajalon.

AZZATI, or KHAZATI, is probably Gaza, as it was with Yafa guarded by Yabitiri. Possibly, however, Ashdod might be considered.

BIDUNA is quite unknown.

BIKHISHI. Only in letter 118, which was written from some place in touch with Nazareth and Jordan region, but quite safe, probably Akka. Bikhishi should be near there and open to the Egyptians; possibly El Bahjeh, 2 N.E. of Akka, remembering the confusion of *j* and *sh* which exists.

BIRUNA, BIRUTA, is well known as Beyrut now.

BITARTI, unknown, probably between Tsumura and Gubla.

BIT NINIB. (1) Near Gubla (203), after Tsumura was lost; unknown. (2) Near Qilti (Keilah), toward Jerusalem (256); unknown.

BIT-TIRI. Occupied by Khaiapa in retreat from Tsumura (?); probably *Kh. et Tireh* on foot of hills 7 S.E. of Akka.

BUR[QA]. Perhaps Bene-beraq, 5 E. of Joppa, as the other names with it in 257 agree with this region.

BURZILIM, near Gubla; unknown.

BUZRUNA, certainly Bozrah by the connection.

DANUNA, certainly Danyaan Heb., *Kh. Dâniân* now, on the headland of Ras en Nakurah at the Tyrian Steps. It is named by Abimilki of Tyre, at a time when he was besieged; it is visible, as the headland to the south, from Tyre.

DIMASHQA, also written Timashgi, is Tamesqu of the Egyptians, *Dimishq*, Damascus.

DUBU, quite unknown, may read Gubbu.

GADASHUNA has been connected with Kitsuna of the Upper Ruten list of Tahutmes III. This latter is Tell Keisan, 6 S.E. of Akka, as fixed by connection with other names.

GAGAYA is connected to Khanigalbat (far N. Syria) and Ugarit (Orontes mouth).

GAR, see ADURI.

GAZRI, Gezer, 20 S.E. of Joppa.

GIMTI is probably distinct from Ginti-kirmil; in 233 Ginti is destroyed, in 256 Gimti is part of the enemies' forces; Ginti, moreover, is qualified by *Kirmil* when it occurs. Gimti is joined with Gezer and Keilah in attacks on the land of Jerusalem, and is probably in the same region as those places. This answers well to Gimzo, Heb. *Jimzu*, 16 S.E. of Joppa, nearly half-way to Jerusalem.

GINA, in south Palestine, probably *Janiah*, 7 W. of Bethel.

GINTI-KIRMIL. As this name merely means "the gardens of the vineyard," like the "gardens," Nos. 44, 63, 70, and 93 in Tahutmes III. list (*History* ii.), it cannot be certainly identified. From the geography it cannot have anything to do with Mount Carmel, as has been absurdly supposed. Its place was somewhere in the approaches to Jerusalem, and west of a "land of Shiri" (234). Some presumption may exist for seeing in this Ginti, En Gannim Heb., "the gardens," now *Kh. Umm Jina* (16 W. Jerusalem); the *kirmil*, "vineyard," is certainly a pre-Hebrew form, as it appears as a loan in Egyptian, *Qirama*, a vineyard, and the form with terminal *l* appears in S. Palestine as Carmel, *Kurmul* (7 S. Hebron). That Gannim should have the adjective *kirmil* is most probable, as it is in the vale of Sorek, "of the choice vine." The connection with the land of Shiri, which would lie on the Jerusalem side of it, points to Shaaraim, *Kh. es Saireh*, 4 E. of it. Letter 234 then would say from Jerusalem that the hills of Shaaraim (12 W. of Jerusalem) were lost as far as En Gannim in the valley of the vine, 4 miles further out.

GITI-RIMUNA occurs in 257 with places near Joppa, agreeing with Gath-rimmon of Jos. xix. 45.

GIZZA was ravaged by Itakama, who came down the Litany valley (see AMKI), and was near *Abdeh*, 15 S. Tyre (see ABITU); it was a fortress occupied by Aziru's troops. All this agrees to the fort of Giscala, *El Jish*, 22 S.E. Tyre.

GUBBU, see DUBU.

GUBLA. This very important place has been assumed to be the same as Gebal, Byblos, *Jebail* (24 S. Tripoli), while another equally likely, Jebel, or "mountain," is at Gabula, *Jibleh*, or *Jebeleh* (61 N. Tripoli). In fact the latter name agrees rather better to Gubla. The letters which point rather to the southern *Jebail* are 147, chief of Gubla is living at Zidon; 197, Ribadda cannot occupy Tsumura because Gubla is surrounded; 202, 207, 209, only Gubla and Beyrut are left; 211, 216, 220, Ribadda left Gubla and went to Beyrut. But, on the other hand, none of these preclude the northern *Jibleh*, and the following all point to that; 152, Khatti plunder round Gubla, early in the break-up; 162, Ambi (= Baldeh ?), Shigata (= Saukat), Ullaza (= El Usy) are lost, and Gubla is in danger; 163, 189, 204 Gubla gets food from Yarimuta (= Laodicea); 189, kings of Mitani and Naharaina are hostile, which is more probable in a northern site. Here Yarimuta is really a key to the question. No such place has yet been noted. Yerimoth, Heb., is impossible, as it was inland. But it is obvious that Yerimoth, Arimathea, Ramoth, Ramah, are all the same name, "the high place," and we must expect to find many such place-names. There is no name like this along the coast near the southern *Jebail;* yet it is certain, from the continual sale of timber and slaves from Gubla, that Yarimuta must have been an important port near Gubla. But on turning to the northern *Jibleh* we see that the next port to that is Laodicea, formerly Ramitha. Here then is a Ramoth or Yerimoth exactly in the required relation to Jibleh. Such a series of names on the coast as Ramitha, Saukat, and El Usy, for Yarimuta, Shigata, and Ullaza, all near the northern *Jibleh* or *Jebeleh*, stamp that as the true Gubla. There are constructions and antiquities, and the harbour has several piers of huge stones, some 11 feet in length (Baedecker), so the conditions for a former city and port are quite fulfilled.

IGAID is unknown. It occurs in the travels of the Mohar in the order Kheta (Hittites), Aupa (Ubi, plain of Damascus), Khaduma (="a fortress"?), Ygatiy, Za . . . (Tyre?)

of king Sesisu (Sesostris = Ramessu II.), Khal . . . or Khar . . . , Qedesh (by Lake Merom), Tubakhi (Kh. et Tubukah, 14 E. Nakura), the Shasu (or Bedawin), Pamagar (Magoras, = Nahr Beyrut?). This points to its being in the north between Damascus and Tyre of Ramessu II. The mountains of Igaid are therefore Lebanon or Anti-Lebanon ; and on the pass over the Lebanon from Damascus to Beyrut is *Ain Yakut*, which may preserve the name.

IRQATA, well known as Arkas (Tell Arqa), 14 E.N.E. Tripoli.

KARDUNIYASH, the official name of the Babylonian kingdom.

KASH is usually supposed to be the same as the land of the Kassi or Babylonians. But in letters 162 and 172 it is linked with Mitani as urging on Aziri. In 193 and 214 men of Kashi are asked for to defend Gubla. In 234 Naharain and Kash are both together within reach of Egyptian ships. In 254 the Kashi fight near Jerusalem. The Kashi were then on the Mediterranean coast near Mitani, and were auxiliary troops of Egyptians. Babylonia is quite impossible, and we are led to the Ugarit region on Orontes as most likely. There Mount Kasios looks down on the Orontes mouth, and seems to retain the name of Kash.

KHABIRI. This name, which merely means "confederates," has been conjectured to refer to the Hebrews. But we find them first invading Ubi (Damascus) and Ashteroth, and in alliance with Abdashirta. This points to their coming in about the middle of Syria, and not from the south, which seems to have been the Hebrew way. It seems quite possible that Hebron was named after them.

KHALUNNI is connected with Bozrah, in the region of Golan ; and though Khalunni would normally remain as Holan, yet as there is some variation in what seem to be forms of this name, Golan for the city and region, and 'Allân for the river traversing it, Khalunni may well represent the original name, which has been modified to Golan and 'Allan by later peoples.

KHARABU, named with places near Joppa, may be *El Khurab* (11 E. Joppa); but perhaps it is only a generic name for a ruin.

KHANIGALBAT is supposed to be the same region as Mitani, which is in Naharaina, or northern Mesopotamia. It was certainly the land of Dushratta's residence. (See letter 11.)

KHASHABU (see AMKI) is the river Hôshaba, the valley of Banias, and very possibly an earlier name of that town.

KHATAT, a district which seems to be not far from Tsumura, yet it is named by people of Tunip. Possibly it is the Lebanon region, connected with the district *El Hadith* near the cedars.

KHATTI are certainly the Khita of the Egyptians, or Hittites. They began to act far in the north, and gradually pushed southwards.

KHAWINI is *Kh. Kâáûn*, 6 S. Bethshean. (See ADURI.)

KHAZATI is Gaza.

KHAZI is *Kh. el 'Azziyeh* (20 E. Tyre). (See AMKI.)

KHAZURA occurs in 70, 71, but only has any position shown in 183, where news of its defection is given from Tyre, with news of Uzu (Hosah) and Zidon. It was thus near Tyre, and doubtless Hazor, 11 S.E. of Tyre.

KHIKUBTA is named as being obviously the king's, and is probably Ha-ka-ptah = Memphis.

KHINATUNA was in the land of Kinakhi, and messengers were on the way there from Babylonia to Egypt, and were attacked from Samkhuna (Merom) and Akka. It was therefore east of the Jordan opposite Merom (124). This agrees to Kenath, Heb., Kanatha, now Kanawat.

KHINIANABI, perhaps Hananieh, *Kefr 'Anân* (12 N.W. Tiberias). (See ADURI.)

KINANAT is agreed to be the name Kanaan. From Qatna by Damascus Akizzi reports that Nukhashi, Ni, Zinzar, and Kinanat are faithful. The "lowland" indicated by this Kinanat is probably, therefore, the head plain of the Orontes, which leads down to near *Shinshâr*, Zinzar.

KINAKHI included the Hauran, as Kanatha was in it (124), and it sent to Mesopotamia to revolt (20). But it seems to have extended right across Syria, as Tyre refers to an officer in Kinakhi (183), and answers about Kinakhi by reporting about Danuna

(178). It must, therefore, be a belt across Galilee to the Hauran.

KINZA, probably in the Baalbek region now lost in one of the Kneseh (church) names. (See AMKI.) It certainly is not Gizza, *Gish* (as has been stated), for the prince of Kinza took Gish (116).

KUATSBAT was probably in the south, and seems to be Chozeba, Heb. *Kh Kueiziba*, 3 N.E. of Halhul.

KUMIDI sent news of Bashan, Damascus, and Galilee (116); but was hopeless after the fall of Tsumura (199). This points to somewhere between Damascus and Tsumura, and agrees to *Kamid el Lauz*, 29 S.E. Beyrut, 31 W.N.W. Damascus, an excellent position to command the upper Litâny basin, and on the old Beyrut-Damascus road of Tahutmes III.

LAKISH was in the south, and is doubtless Lachish.

LAPANA was attacking Qatna near Damascus; probably Helbon, 13 N.W. Damascus.

LUKKI are a people who professed alliance with Cyprus, but attacked and plundered there, and were repudiated by the Alashiyans.

This leaves no doubt that they are the Luka or Lykians who appear as sea-rovers in the next two dynasties.

MAGDALI, in 118, is probably the Migdol ("tower") of Magdala (3 N.W. Tiberias). (See ADURI.) In 262 it is a tower in the south near Kuatsbat.

MAGIDDA is certainly Megiddo; and by the campaign of Tahutmes III. it is clear that this is at *Tell el Mutasellim*, and not at *Kh. el Mujedda*, though the latter was very likely a colony of Megiddo, as *Umm Lakis* was a colony of Lachish (Tell el Hesy).

MAKHZI . . . TI, not identified; see USHTIRU: perhaps the same as MIKHIZA.

MANKHATISHUM was in the south, not far from Gezer (260). The Wady Menakh (7 S. Gezer) seems to preserve the name.

MIKHIZA was the city of Arzawaya (75), evidently another reading of Rukhizi (112). This is probably on the south side of Hermon, as Arzawiya fought in Upper Galilee (116), attacked Namyawaza of Kumidi when he went into Damascus (116), and was leagued with Itakama and Helbon against Katana.

MILUKHA. The men of Milukha were auxiliaries of the Egyptians, and are thrice asked for by Ribaddi. As they were probably coast Syrians, it is not improbable that they were Tyrian troops, named from *Kh. el Maluhiyeh* 4 S.E. of Tyre. *Kh* usually softens to *h* in modern forms.

MISHTU, *Mushta* (14 W. Tiberias) see ADURI.

MITANI is Aram Naharaim, or upper Mesopotamia.

MU . . KHAZI was near Gezer (237); possibly *Kh. el Mukheizin*, 8 S.W. Gezer.

MUSHIKHUNA occupied by a ruler Shutarna ; neither name occurs again.

NARIMA, NAAKHRIMA, the country of Naharain by Mitani, in upper Mesopotamia.

NAZIMA, unknown, and without any clue.

NI, probably the same as the Egyptian possession Niy. By one reference (*Hist.* ii. 63) it looks as if it were in Naharaina, but this is explained by a similar passage (*Hist.* 116), where after setting up a tablet in Naharaina, the king came to the city of Niy in going south, after the tablet was set

N

up. Niy is linked with Senzaru, Zinzar of these letters, *Shinshar*, 10 m. S. Homs (*Hist.* 123). Elephants were hunted in Niy (*Hist.* 124); and this shows that there must have been fertile plains. It is linked with Ammiya and Ardata (letter 187), and so might be possibly *Niha*, 15 S.W. of Baalbek: on the other hand it is referred to by the men of Tunip (letter 170), which points rather to *Kefr Naya*, 8 W.N.W. of Aleppo, and this would better fit the week's march of Amenhotep II. to Ugarit.

NINA, city of Ishtar, is Nineveh.

NUKHASHI. This is the name of an important country of N. Syria. It has been strangely confused with Anaugasa of Tahutmes III. annals. (*Hist.* 110, 117, 120.) Anaugasa is connected with Zahi (Phœnicia), and in its first mention is placed among three country palaces of the king of Megiddo, Yenuamu, Anaugasa, and Harnekaru. These should be found near together, and somewhere within the territories of Megiddo. Yenuamu appears to be Yanuh (7 E. Tyre), Yanu of the Amu or Syrians, for the latter part of the name is spelled in some cases exactly as the Amu. Harnekaru seems almost certainly the Har or hill of Nekaru, now *Nakura*, the great headland of the Scala Tyriorum (12 m. S. Tyre), Nakura and Yanuh and by streams, and Anaugasa between them would probably be on the intermediate stream of the Wady 'Ezziyeh. It is just possible that Anaugasa has been corrupted into Medinet en Nahas (city of brass) on that stream. Anyhow this dependency, or country palace, of the king of Megiddo can have nothing to do with the far northern kingdom of Nukhashi. Nukhashi appears to have been between the Orontes and Euphrates, from the various mentions of it.

QANU, from the prince of which a letter remains (44), might be "the water of Qina," by Megiddo of the Tahutmes campaign (*Hist.* ii. 107), or *Qana*, 8 S.E. of Tyre, or Cana — *Qanet el Jelil* — 13 W. Tiberias. There is nothing to prove the position.

QATNA we have seen to be Qatana, 14 W.S.W. of Damascus. (See AMKI.)

QIDESHU was the patrimony of Itakama (114), and probably Qedesh by Lake Homs.

Qidsha, of 147, seems to be probably the same Qedesh.

QILTI is usually recognized as *Keilah*, 8 N.W. of Hebron.

QUTU was near Ardata and Irqata, but is now unknown.

RUBUTA is a Rabbath or capital, and was near Gezer (260) and not far from Gimzu and Keilah (256). This points to *Kh. Rubba* (4 N.N.W. Keilah), supposed to be Rabbah of Josh. xv. 60.

RUKHIZI, see MIKHIZA.

SHADDU was near Gizza, *Gish*, and Abitu, *Abdeh ;* perhaps *Shatiyeh*, 6 S.E. of Tyre.

SHAMKHUNA was the city of Shumaddu, who leagued with Akku to attack Kanawat in the Hauran. Between these two places is Lake Merom, known as Semekhonitis in Greek times, with the *'Ain es Semakh*, 6 N.E. of the lake.

SHANKHAR was allied with the Khatti, in relation to Alashiya. Probably the Egyptian Senzar or Sangar. Whether it be the same as ZINZAR, *Shinshar* (11 S. Homs), or be *Sejar* (13 N.W. Homs), is not clear.

SHANKU, near Irqata ; apparently *Shaqqa* on the coast 10 S.W. of Tripoli.

SHASKHIMI, city of Abdimilki, not identified.

SHIGATA is Tell Saukat or Sukat, 3 m. S. of *Jebeleh*, see GUBLA.

SHIKHLALI would be found now most likely as Sihlali, and this might well be a *sahel* or plain on the coast near Tsumura, with which it is mentioned.

SHIRDANA are named as Egyptian auxiliaries, and are doubtless the Shardana, foreign auxiliaries so well known in the XIXth Dynasty.

SHIRI, Shaaraim, Heb. *Kh. es Saireh* (12 W. Jerusalem), see GINTI KIRMIL.

SHUARBI would be very important to identify, as (216) it was "the gate to Gubla," but it cannot be found on maps either by Jebail or Jebeleh.

SHUNA[MA ?], perhaps *Selmeh* (3 E. Joppa), as it was in that neighbourhood.

SUARTI ? or BITARTI unidentified, probably between Tsumura and Gubla.

SUBARI, a land perhaps between Mitani and the Hauran. Perhaps *Seburra*, 37 E. Laodicea (Baedecker).

Suri, a district not far from Tsumura; possibly the region *Esh Shara*, 15 E. of Tsumura.

Suti, the Sati of the Egyptians, Bedawin of S.E. Syria.

Takh . . . . not far from Megiddo, very possibly the same as

Takhida, to which a messenger from Tsumura to Egypt reached, but could not get through; therefore on the Egyptian road. The name is not now found.

Tana or Tashu not identified. Possibly Denniyeh, district east of Tripolis.

Taruna has no localization. Possibly *Toran*, 10 W. Tiberias.

Timashgi, see Dimashqa, is undoubtedly Tamesqu of Egyptians. *Dimeshk*, Damascus.

Tsapuna was in the south, as Ayalon and Zorah are mentioned by the ruler. The name corresponds to Siffîn (9 E. of Ludd) of Baedecker, but the Exploration Society's map gives the name as *Shebtîn*.

Tsarkha, named with Ayalon from Tsapuna, is doubtless Tsor'ah, Heb., now Tsur'ah, 6 S. Ayalon, 15 E. of Jerusalem,

TSARKHI, probably a *zerga* or dark place, in the Jordan valley, see ADURI.

TSIDUNA is certainly Zidon.

TSUMUR is certainly Simyra, now *Sumra*, as all the indications agree. The refusal to agree to this, because the Assyrian spelling, six centuries later, was Zimarra, is altogether hypercritical, when we see the free variations in rendering many important names in both cuneiform and Egyptian.

TSURRI is certainly *Tsur*, Tyre.

TUBIKHI has no indication of locality, but agrees in name with Debkhu of the list of Tahutmes III. (No. 6 Upper Ruten) which is either *Et Tabghah* on N.W. of Sea of Galilee, or *Jebel Tubakat*, 7 N.W. of that.

TUMURKHA was in the south, being named with Gezer and Rabbah and Mankhatishum (Wady Menakh). It agrees thus well to *Tumrah* (7 N.E. of Gaza); *kh* usually softening to *h*.

TUNIP is generally agreed with good reason to be *Tennib* (18 N. of Aleppo). It appears to have had the importance which Aleppo has possessed in later times; this may well be, as it was on the road from the plain of Antioch to the ruling kingdom of Mitani, while Aleppo was on the line to the later centre of rule, Babylon, lower down the Euphrates.

TUSHULTI attacked Khazi, *Kh. el'Azziyeh* (20 E. Tyre). This makes it almost impossible to be Tasuret, of Tahutmes Upper Ruten list No. 56, as that belongs to the region of Shechem, and is almost certainly Teiasir, 11 N.E. of Shechem. No name corresponds with this near el 'Azziyeh ; but there is a bare possibility that an inversion might have occurred in the cuneiform, or in subsequent history, and that *Talluseh*, 5 S.W. of el 'Azziyeh, might be the site.

UBI, a district in which was Damascus, evidently the plain of Damascus.

UDUMU, Adameh, Heb. *Damieh*, 5 S.W. of Tiberias, see ADURI.

UGARIT, a district in the north of Syria, on the coast (letter 152 ; news obtained by sea, letter 178), and far north, at the limits of Egyptian claims (letter 171). The only valuable piece of country on the coast north of Gubla is the mouth of the Orontes, which must have been of importance, and is not otherwise mentioned. Looking down on this is *Jebel Okrad*, which seems like Ugarit, but which only means the mountain of the Kurds (pl. *Okrad* or *Akrad*). There is, however, a possibility that as the Kurds, or Carduchi, were in Greek times much where they are now, this Kurd mountain might have been thus named as early as these letters, and the land of Ugarit might be the land of Okrad or the Kurds. The indications fix it pretty clearly without any identification of the name.

ULLAZA, a port near Tsumura, probably *Mina Kabusi*, behind which is *El Usy:* see AMBI.

URUSALIM, generally agreed to be Jerusalem.

USHTIRU was probably in the upper part of the Litany valley, as it was on the route of the northern enemy approaching Khazi, *el 'Azziyeh* (letter 252). This would agree well to *Shtora*, 21 E. Beyrut, on the Damascus road.

USU or Uzu was close to Tyre and agrees with Hosah, Heb. *'Ezziyeh*, 6 S. of Tyre.

WURZA has no locality shown, but may well be Kh. Yerzeh, 11 N.E. Shechem.

YABISHI is Yabesh Gilead, 12 S.E. Bethshean; see ADURI.

YADA comes after Ambi, Shigata, and Ullaza, but no modern name thereabouts resembles it.

YAPU is certainly *Yafa* or Joppa.

YARIMUTA cannot be the Biblical Yerimoth, as that was inland; but Yerimoth, Arimathea, Ramoth, and Ramah, are all terms for a high place, and may occur anywhere. The best indication is that it was an important port of commerce, and close to Gubla. The nearest port to Gabula is Laodicea, and as this was a Ramoth, being known as Ramitha, it is pretty certainly Yarimuta; see GUBLA.

YIBULIYA must be between Gubla, where Ribadda was, and Tsumura, to which his man was going when captured (letter 161): no such name is in the map.

YIKHLIYA is linked with Ullaza, Ardata, Y., Ambi, and Shigata; it is probably *Qleiát*, 5 N.E. of Ardata.

YINUAMMA is the Egyptian Yenuamu, or Yanoah, Heb. *Yanuh*, 7 E. Tyre, belonging to the Amu or Syrians.

ZALUKHI was a coast land near Ugarit, not identified.

ZIKHRA a city of Alashiya or Cyprus, exposed to Lycian incursions.

ZILU was in the south, named next after Ginti (En Gannim); it may well be Zelah, Heb., N. of Jerusalem, but not identified.

ZINZAR is named between Ni and Kinanat, and can hardly be other than *Shinshar*, 11 S. of Homs.

ZIRIBASHANI is the plain of Bashan.

ZUKHLI is named as a city of Egypt, where a messenger would find the king. This was probably a capital city, and in lower Egypt. It can hardly be other than Memphis, the city of Ptah Sokar, now Saqqara. The constant mutation of *l* and *r* in Egyptian prevent any difficulty in this identification.

PLYMOUTH :
WILLIAM BRENDON AND SON,
PRINTERS.

For EU product safety concerns, contact us at Calle de José Abascal, 56–1°, 28003 Madrid, Spain or eugpsr@cambridge.org.

www.ingramcontent.com/pod-product-compliance
Ingram Content Group UK Ltd.
Pitfield, Milton Keynes, MK11 3LW, UK
UKHW012345130625
459647UK00009B/536